W9-BAQ-135

A 10/17/73
9971402

HUNTING BIG GAME
IN THE CITY PARKS

Howard G. Smith

Illustrated by Anne Marie Jauss

ABINGDON PRESS

Nashville   *New York*

Copyright © 1969 by Howard G. Smith
All rights reserved
Printed in the United States of America
Library of Congress Catalog Card Number: 69-10616

To Hsing-Hua, Wei-Hsin, Ricky, and Li-Hsin
—my four adventurers

Contents

1
The Backyard Safari: An Introduction to Adventure

If you were to fly over an unexplored African forest in a helicopter, you could expect to see little more than a few brightly colored birds and the tops of thousands of trees. And if you continued on over the dusty African plains, you would still see only little more than patches of dry grass, an occasional muddy waterhole, and one or two small herds of zebras or Thompson's gazelles. You would soon learn that the only way to see the fascinating wild creatures of Africa is to come down to the level at which they live and love, hunt and fight. Only when you become a part of the life that you are watching will you be able to see the eager leopard crouched in wait, the nervous impala the leopard is stalking, or the pride of lions lying lazily in the shade of a grove of acacia trees at midday.

If you were flying to a safari headquarters where an experienced hunter was waiting, you would find that even he needs a guide and tracker who knows the animals and the forests as well as he knows his own friends and village. The guide's lifelong knowledge of the habits of the wild creatures would make your hunt much easier because he would be able to tell you where to look and what to look for when you got there.

But if you are looking for exciting and mysterious animals, it is not necessary to go all the way to Africa to find them. In the shadowy forests of weeds and wild flowers near your own home you will find strange, armored monsters who hunt by moonlight and whose mighty jaws are capable of crushing their prey in an instant. In the city parks or in nearby woodlands you will find quiet, hidden streams and shaded ponds whose murky waters conceal weird creatures that are hungrier and more daring than crocodiles. On the nearest baseball diamond you will find the miniature dusty plains and sunbaked deserts across which you may one day watch an army of slave-hunting Amazon ants marching off to war. In a patch of clover waving gently in a summer breeze you may find the deadly bee wolf lying in ambush as its innocent honeybee prey darts within range.

Though practically all these creatures live within walking distance of your own home, it is doubtful that you have seen more than a very few of them. Even then you probably did not know what you were seeing. There is a knack to finding this type of big game, but it is not a very difficult one. All you need is to know where to look and what to look for when you get there.

In the chapters to come you will be shown not only how to find these wild creatures, but also how to capture them for a really wild wildlife zoo or even for mounting as trophies! Your weapons and traps will be easy to make, but you will also need a good tracker. Since you can't very easily make one of those, it will be up to you to stalk these animals. Once you become familiar with their natural habits in the wild, you will be able to organize a safari that will bring you the kind of hunting experiences that less adventurous people only dream about.

If you are content to look down on the insect world from the safety of a sidewalk or park bench you cannot expect to see much of interest. But when you actually travel out into the world of the insects, you will find an unending story of adventure and mystery. These small but often aggressive creatures must go forth each day in search of food. Quite often they themselves serve as food for some stronger or more ferocious creatures. This strange and frightening world knows no peace and freedom from hunger. Each day brings new troubles and mortal danger in many forms.

But how are you to travel on safari into this magic world of insects? Is it necessary to use your imagination and pretend all this? Not at all! Have you ever seen a brightly colored grasshopper munching on a tender blade of grass in early spring? Have you ever watched a bumblebee riding a daisy to the ground as it bends beneath her bulky body? At times such as these you have been at the edge of this world, though not quite inside it. The next time you come to a patch of tall grass or a little bed of clover or wild flowers, lie down in it and look over the beckoning tips of the grassblades. If the day is young, watch the sunlight striking diamonds from the sparkling dew drops or take a really close look at the magnificent detail of a single flower. You will find beauty and color that you never knew existed. If the weather is warm, you can lie on your back and watch the clouds drifting high above the buzz of foraging insects busy with their unceasing search for food. Suddenly you find yourself in another world. You see for the first time how high and forbidding are the weed forests, how inviting the perfume of the clover, how delicately formed the tiny wild flowers that you have never noticed before. You can smell the dampness of the cool soil as the warming sun draws forth the mist that has lain on it since the previous evening. You will begin to realize that the word "dirt" is a poor description of the soil which is actually a quite wonderful mixture of powdered leaves and dried grass, tiny plant stems, bits of seed husks, minute grains of sand, and other minerals, some of which have blown from across the continent in ages past.

When you arise from this tiny insect jungle, see if you can find a moss-covered rock or a patch of moss in the shadow of an old log. Now take a closer look at it than you ever have before. It is not enough to look at it from three or four feet away and shrug your shoulders because there is nothing there to see. Get a good magnifying glass and lie down in the grass with it. Look at the moss from a distance of three or four inches, using the magnifying glass to pick out the tiny details.

In one small patch of moss you will find hundreds of delicate little stems bearing many leaves so tiny that they are almost invisible. Sometimes you may find that your patch of moss resembles a tiny forest of pine trees growing on a prehistoric mountainside. Still another patch may bear fragile little blossoms too tiny for the smallest honeybee to alight upon. Yet if you are patient and look still more closely, you may find a beetle or other tiny insect hiding beneath the cover of what appears to him to be a great forest. You will find the powdery remains of dead moss leaves lying beneath the living plants and perhaps even bits of oak leaves that once covered the entire patch.

Sometimes on a hot summer night a ponderous old rhinoceros beetle

9

rhinoceros beetle (haircap moss, pixie cups)

prowling the darkness may crush the delicate stems of the same moss forest you are examining. Beneath his monstrous, thundering feet, the much tinier beetles of the moss will lie quivering with fear until the terrible stranger has passed and all is quiet once again.

If you still have some time after leaving the moss forest, why not take your first good look at the remarkable community in and under a rotted log or decaying tree stump? Have you ever taken the time before now to examine the brightly colored mushrooms and delicate, mossy lichens that grow on its shady side where the air remains cool and moist all day? When you find one while on safari, pull away a small strip of crumbling bark, and you will quite likely get a glimpse of beetles and spiders scurrying for cover. Turn the log over, and you will see earthworms, millipedes ("thousand-leggers"), and beetle larvae ("grubworms") living in shallow burrows almost in the middle of a nest of red ants. You will see the ant nurses hurrying away into the forbidding depths of their dark tunnels, carrying the little white ant larvae (grubs) and pupae (young ants still in the cocoon). Even as the nurses hurry away with the helpless babies, the warriors and other workers are dashing frantically about, searching for the dangerous enemy that has threatened their home. The first earthworm or beetle larva that they meet will get the blame for turning the log over, and they will make quick work of him. Inside the log itself are thousands of tunnels and galleries housing full-grown beetles, little red spiders, certain types of young wasps, and miniature greenhouses filled with lacy molds and glistening spider webs. You may even find a colony of termites which will quickly die if they remain exposed to the dry air outside the log.

Some of the strange creatures that you discover will have lived their entire lives inside this old log, while others use it as a shelter during the day and venture forth at night to make raids on their neighbors. Some of them steal their neighbors' stored food, while others carry off the neighbors!

Of course these are only a few of many hundreds of places in which you will make fascinating discoveries among the wildlife of this unusual new world. Every rock, every tree, and almost every clump of grass or slender weed stem has a different story to tell. The rocks become mighty

11

mountains, often covered with tiny forests. The trees become a world within themselves, housing some of the most colorful and interesting living things in the world. The clumps of grass become tangled jungles, the weed stems the trunks of ancient trees. Here you will witness the wonders of the strangest creatures alive. You will see them as they eat or as they simply sit in the sunshine half asleep while nearby there may be a fierce battle raging between two male crickets or between a tiger beetle and a tent caterpillar. You will see well-organized battles between warring tribes of ants, or perhaps you will witness the vicious attack of an aphis lion on a herd of honey-producing aphids. At the edge of a miniature desert you will see a hardworking red ant suddenly drop out of sight as she falls into the merciless jaws of the ant lion who lies in ambush at the bottom of a sand trap.

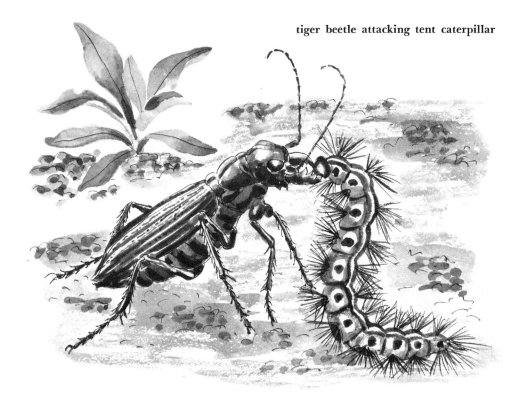

tiger beetle attacking tent caterpillar

However, you cannot expect these creatures to be lined up in your backyard waiting for you to examine them. Often you must search for days or weeks before you find some of them where they are supposed to be. You might just as often find them where they are never supposed to be, too. But when the day comes in which you are unable to find anything of interest no matter how hard you look, then you will know how the professional hunter feels when he must tell his eager clients that he really has no idea why the lions aren't where they are supposed to be. They may have been coming to the same waterhole for years, but there will be times when they simply refuse to show up. At least your safari isn't costing you a hundred dollars a day!

On the other hand, if the lions could always be depended upon to come to the same spot and stand quietly while they were being shot at by nervous hunters, or if a spider-hunting wasp could be depended upon to fight to the death with a hairy wolf spider while you make yourself comfortable in a pleasant spot, then where is the adventure? Lions can be seen in a zoo, and insects may be viewed in careful displays in a museum. But this is not the way of the big game hunter! Adventure comes at least as much with the search as with the capture.

The first thing you may do after reading this chapter will be to dash outdoors and run all over your backyard looking for some of these armored monsters, green cattle, pirates, and flying wolves. If you do, you may be just as disappointed as the inexperienced African big game hunter who snatches up a loaded rifle and dashes out of safari headquarters looking for something to shoot. When he gets tired and comes back inside, he will find the professional hunter and his native trackers hiding under the bed. The eager hunter will find that if he gives them a sporting chance, the professional hunter and his trackers will be happy to show him where to hunt and what to look for when he gets there. In a similar manner you will find that you will enjoy your own hunts more if you give this guidebook a sporting chance to help you get started.

The author once had occasion to contact a large safari headquarters in India in an attempt to locate a pair of tiger cubs for a client. They were very helpful, but they simply could not produce tigers with just a couple of days' notice. Their professional hunters knew that tigers as well as a variety of big game animals were in the surrounding jungles. But in order to locate the tigers in the shortest time possible, they said that they would have to send out trackers to look just for tigers while ignoring other game animals. You will probably find it best to begin your safaris in the same way. First decide what you are stalking, make sure that it can be found in hunting territory similar to yours, then make up your mind to ignore lesser prey. There will always be unexpected adventures on any safari, but not enough of them to make a satisfactory hunt if you just go looking for anything that hops, swims, or crawls.

There is also another very good reason for planning your hunts. If you tried to carry all kinds of collection equipment on every safari, you would find yourself so loaded down that you would not have much of a chance to stalk your prey. The most common items that you will find useful are a lightweight, long-handled net, a pair of long forceps (tweezers), a smooth stick such as a cutoff broomstick, and a flat stick such as a tongue depressor used by a doctor to examine your throat. Other tools that you will almost always want to carry with you will be a magnifying glass and a pocketknife. If you are on a collecting trip, you will need a killing jar and small boxes of dry grass for bringing back undamaged trophies for mounting. If you are hunting animals for your zoo compound, you will need several small jars half-filled with dry grass and covered with gauze or screen wire. You will find more information about the selection and use of collecting tools in a later chapter.

In the chapters to come you will find the life stories of some of the most unusual animals in the world. A few of the species described are rather difficult to find, but most of them should be common to your hunting territory whether it is your own neighborhood or the nearest city park. Of course these are only a few of the ones you will find on your safaris. But when you have mastered the art of stalking these, then you will find it still more exciting to discover for yourself the fascinating life stories of the strangers you meet.

2

Tyrannosaurus Rex
of the Flower Garden

Hidden beneath the protective cover of the climbing roses on the back fence, or gliding silently through a tangled jungle of shasta daisies in the garden are sometimes found the terrible dinosaurs of the insect jungles. Even *Tyrannosaurus rex,* most dreaded of all dinosaurs, would not have had a chance against this expressionless killer if both had been the same size. While *Tyrannosaurus* had fearful, crushing jaws with which to cripple and tear apart its prey, the deadly praying mantis of the insect jungles has a far more dangerous pair of heavily spiked forelegs which can lash out and impale a victim in a fraction of a second. Even such a dangerous creature as the poisonous hornet or a sun-toughened grasshopper with its steel-spring muscles is helpless against the crushing forelegs of the mantis. Just the unexpected appearance of this awesome creature has been known to frighten cats, dogs, and even grown men.

Does such an efficient killer have any enemies from which it will itself shrink in fear when even a vicious dog will flee from it? Yes, but the most unlikely enemy of all is the one that the mantis fears the most. What could this be? A huge, armored stag beetle with its cruel jaws? One of the quick and skillful hunting wasps? No, it is neither of these. The mantis fears only the little red ant which is scarcely an eighth of an inch long. We shall soon see why this is so, even though the ants would rarely if ever even consider attacking a grown mantis.

Whenever I see an ant approaching a mantis, I usually move the frightened mantis. It is the least that I can do to show my gratitude to the mantises after one of them helped me escape from a possible attack by one of the insect jungle's most feared predators. This happened in my own backyard during the last part of June. I had been lying in the grass watching an alligator-shaped aphis lion eating his way through a herd of tiny green aphid cattle on one of my rose bushes. Suddenly my thoughts were rudely interrupted by the curiosity of a large red wasp who insisted on investigating one of my ears. At a time like that it is difficult to remember why I ever considered going on an insect safari. It is about the same feeling that a falconer has when he is hanging from a rope just over an eagle's nest and the mama eagle decides to return home. No matter which way he moves, he knows it will be a waste of time.

At first the wasp hummed over my head in tight circles, coming so close once or twice that she actually touched my ear. After several minutes of lying there paralyzed with uncertainty about the wasp's intentions, I noticed that the buzzing had suddenly become more high pitched and angry. It seemed now that the wasp must have alighted on one of my rose bushes because the sound was no longer moving in circles around my head. Taking advantage of my chance, I desperately rolled over and over, then leaped to my feet several yards away. The wasp didn't follow me. She had problems of her own—fatal problems.

A slender, green creature with gauzy wings spread over her back like sails had pinioned the wasp with sharp spines and barbs of her heavily muscled forelegs. It was the first and certainly the most welcome praying mantis that had visited my garden that year. As the struggles of the wasp became weaker, the mantis carefully closed her wings over her back to give the appearance of a fat but flexible green stick balancing on two pairs of legs. She was using her forelegs only for holding her prey up to her jaws.

By the time I could get close enough to see what was happening, the mantis was daintily eating her way through the armor plate of the wasp's thorax. The wasp didn't think much of this, of course. She was buzzing as hard as she could with the one wing that remained free, and her wicked stinger was being thrust about in every direction in an effort to destroy her captor. None of this disturbed the mantis at all. She just kept on eating until the wasp's struggles grew weaker and finally ceased entirely. In a few minutes the mantis had eaten most of the thorax and abdomen and had dropped the wasp's head, wings, and

16

oriental mantis eating paper wasp

a few other bits onto the ground below the branch on which she sat.

While my unlikely rescuer was casually cleaning her barbed forelegs, I made a careful examination of the ground below the rose stem on which she was perched. It was difficult to identify the remains scattered about, but it appeared that she had eaten at least two wasps, a katydid, and several flies. She must have been on that same perch for at least two days. Apparently the game was plentiful there, so she had been choosy about the parts of her victims that she would eat. In leaner times she would eat everything but the wings.

Though I had not seen the attack, I knew what must have happened. The silly wasp must have either hovered within range of the mantis' forelegs for a fraction of a second, or else she had curiously alighted nearby, and the mantis had crept up on her a step at a time. For the praying mantis, a nice crunchy wasp is nothing more than a spicy meal. She seems to find quite a wide variety of insects and other animals to her liking. She has been known to attack and eat everything from houseflies to small lizards and baby birds. Whether it walks, hops, flies, or slithers along, it's all meat on the table so far as the mantis is concerned.

No insect zoo is complete without one of these dinosaurs in an exhibition cage. Or if you should happen to have a problem with houseflies in the summertime, a mantis hanging on a curtain in your house will be very helpful in getting rid of them. My wife prefers insect spray to praying mantises, so this one went into a terrarium complete with ferns and a half-buried piece of rotted wood that together gave the impression of a small patch of prehistoric forest. The mantis seemed right at home in these surroundings, but she soon became restless and began wandering about over the fern.

At the time I thought that the mantis might simply be lonely in the terrarium by herself, so I spent several hours searching for a companion for her. When I finally located another female in my neighbor's privet hedge, my little captive dinosaur was quick to show her appreciation for my thoughtfulness. She pounced on the newcomer immediately, clamped it in her forelegs, and began eating her unfortunate visitor as casually as she had eaten the wasp that morning.

18

Thinking that this was my own fault for letting her get too hungry before I introduced the other mantis, I caught a half dozen flies, a cricket, and a small grasshopper and dropped them into her terrarium. While she was happily eating her way through this assortment, I scoured the neighborhood for a third mantis. This time my captive was a male, slightly smaller than the female. It was getting late, so I also brought back another grasshopper just in case the female was still hungry.

I dropped both grasshopper and mantis into the terrarium while the female was finishing off the last of her victims. This time I knew that she would be too well fed to pay any particular attention to the second mantis. But the male was hungry, too. He soon captured the grasshopper that had been dropped in the terrarium with him. While he was eating the grasshopper, the female crept up behind both of them and seized the male. You might expect this to result in a fierce fight, but the male mantis was so busy eating his grasshopper that he failed to notice that the female mantis was eating him! The whole thing was too much for me. I took the terrarium outside and dropped the three creatures in the rose garden. The next morning only the fragments of the grasshopper's wings and one foreleg of the male remained on the ground. The female had disappeared.

Those were the last of the praying mantises that I saw in my own neighborhood that year, but late that summer I decided to go hunting for some insect dinosaur eggs. The mantis does not lay her eggs in the open like many of the dinosaurs did. Instead she builds a silken egg case within which she lays several hundred fragile eggs.

It took several days of careful hunting to find just two egg cases. This was about as easy as locating a wounded tiger in a bamboo grove, though I must say that it was quite a lot safer. The egg cases don't scream and pounce on your back when you aren't looking. They are large enough to find easily, but the pecan-shaped nest may vary in color from that of ripe wheat to that of a faded brown hunting boot. They are generally built in a sheltered spot in a sunny location, but may be attached to a stone, a vine, dry grass, strips of old cloth, a brick, or to a tree limb. Practically any support with a rough or uneven surface seems to be quite satisfactory to the mantis. She doesn't have anything to worry about, because her young can take care of themselves almost from the time they emerge in the spring.

During the egg laying, the end of the female's abdomen is embedded in a mass of grayish white, silken foam produced from the tip of her abdomen. She has to work fast because it begins to harden in less than two minutes during which she must construct a layer of the multi-storied egg case and lay her eggs in it. The entire nest is built in horizontal layers that overlap like shingles on a roof. Little paddles protruding from the female's abdomen beat the silk into a froth just like an eggbeater whips egg whites into a thick foam. As the female swings her abdomen from left to right and back again, each swing produces a layer of eggs inside a layer of egg case.

One female must have built both the egg cases that I eventually found in a nearby park. They were attached to thick branches of a wild grapevine, though one was built near the ground and the other was about ten feet above the ground. It was difficult to decide whether I should remove one of the cases and take it home with me. If I left them in the park, they might well be destroyed by field mice or woodpeckers. On the other hand, I have always preferred to study wild creatures under natural conditions, so I finally decided to leave the nests alone.

When I returned to the wild grapevine early in May of the following year, the highest one of the two nests had disappeared. Fortunately, the one near the ground appeared to have been undisturbed. For almost a week I came by to check the nest early each morning. The following Thursday I found tiny fragments of the membranes which had covered the young ones as they began emerging before I had arrived

that morning. This was greatly disappointing, but all was not yet lost. It sometimes takes two days for the egg case to be emptied, so I was there again at daybreak the following morning. Two hours or so later my wait of half a year was at last rewarded.

A short time after my arrival that morning, another delegation arrived to wait for the young mantises. They were just as interested in the emergence as I was, judging from the way they ran up and down the grapevine and out onto the egg case. These unwelcome visitors were a marauding tribe of Argentine ants gathered for a feast of mantis meat.

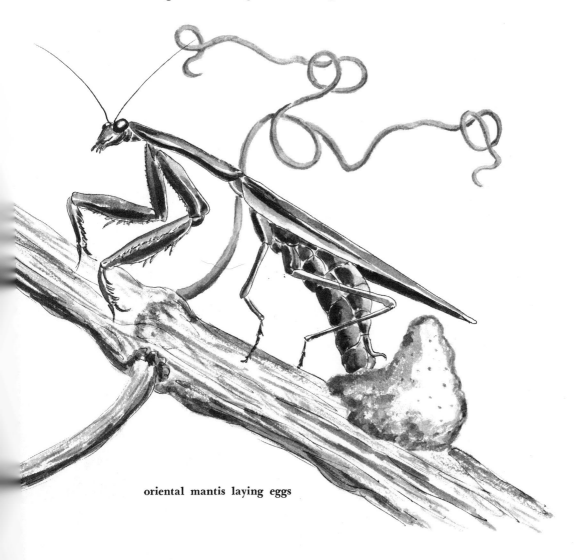

oriental mantis laying eggs

As much as I wanted the young mantises to survive, I was much more likely to learn another of Nature's carefully guarded secrets if I didn't interfere in the battle between the ants and the mantises. Soon the tender-bodied young mantises were pushing their way out of the lower levels of the egg case. As they dangled in a long, moist string that reached the ground, the ants immediately began pouncing on them. Soon there was a long line of ants carrying the fresh, green meat back to the nest. Only a few of the tiny mantises would escape, but it would be enough.

When the baby mantises first emerged from the nest, they were completely enclosed in individual membranes that kept their legs and antennae pressed close to the body. Those that escaped the ants by falling to the ground were also soon able to escape the imprisoning membrane by twisting and swelling until the moist covering dried out and split down the middle. The survivors of the massacre then drew themselves out of the skin and cautiously moved away from the area.

Early that afternoon I returned to the park and made a careful search of the ground. The three survivors that had remained in the vicinity of the grapevine had already developed the hard, protective coating that would make them unappetizing to any scouting ants. In fact one or two ants accidentally stumbled into one of the little mantises, but they quickly scurried away as the little beast reared up on its hind legs and drew its forelegs up into a fighting position. The ants would never again dare to attack these survivors, but the mantises could never forget the terrible morning in which so many of their brothers and sisters had perished in the jaws of the ants. They would fear the now harmless enemies for the rest of their lives.

Yet, even as I was feeling sorry for these monstrous little babies, one of them grabbed its sister and made a meal of her on the spot.

Hunting Guide
Scientific Name: (1) *Tenodera*—the oriental mantis; (2) *Stagmomantis*—the native American mantis.

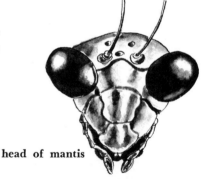

head of mantis

Common Names: devil's horse, soothsayer, praying mantis, devil's rearhorse, praying flower, mule-killer.

Description: *Tenodera* is a bright green color. A full grown adult may be four inches long.

Stagmomantis, sometimes known as the Carolina mantis, is about two inches long when full grown. Its color is green and brown. Several other native species are brown and gray.

Habitat: The oriental mantis was accidentally imported from Asia in 1896. It has since spread all over southeastern North America and has migrated as far west as Arizona.

The Carolina mantis is found from New York and New Jersey west to southern Indiana, Utah, Arizona, and all through the Gulf States.

Stalking Methods: Only the males have wings strong enough for short flights, while the females must depend upon their four walking legs. Thus mantises do not move either very far or very fast. You will usually find them sitting rigid as a statue on a low tree branch, on a twig in a hedge, or on a flower stem. They may be found from May until the first killing frost of the autumn. Unless you find an egg case early in May, your chances of locating young ones this early in the year are very slight. Even the adults are difficult to locate because of their natural coloring and their slow movements. As would be true in the case of all meat-eating insects, you will find them mainly in the vicinity of flowers and pools of water that would be attractive to large numbers of other insects.

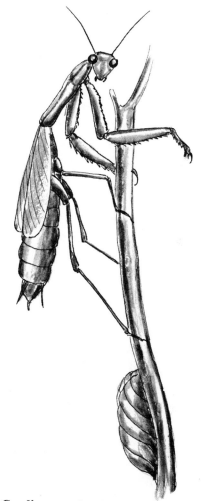

Carolina mantis with egg case

3
Pirates and Kidnappers

The Terrible Bee Wolf

Though it sometimes took weeks to locate a particular kind of big game insect, there was always enough wildlife in the fields and thickets at just one edge of my favorite park to make any hunt a rewarding adventure. In fact many such adventures were the result of completely accidental discoveries.

One morning early in August, while searching for the nest of a praying mantis, I stumbled onto a pirates' nest of the ferocious black and yellow wasps known as bee wolves. That day my search had been at the edge of a field of clover that abruptly broke off on one side to form a sloping limestone cliff. The other three sides were bordered by a thicket of sumac, honeysuckle, and blackberry briars. It was at the edge of this thicket that I first saw a bee wolf attacking its prey.

One of the hundreds of golden honeybees in the small field had been working a patch of clover near my feet while I stood there rather absent-mindedly watching her. She had picked up so much of the sparkling nectar and sticky pollen that she seemed hardly able to lift herself from the last blossom. As she rose into the air to start back toward the hive, a bee wolf sprang at her from ambush.

The frightened bee veered away and tried to take cover in a tuft of foxtail grass at the edge of the thicket, but the bee wolf was even faster. She had already struck the bee with her poisonous sting before it could hide. The terrified bee fought back with fierce courage, but her venomous stinger only glanced off of the tough shell of her enemy. A moment later the wolf struck again, this time reaching a vital spot in the bee's tender neck. The battle ended at once.

Since this had taken place almost under my feet, I could easily watch the bee wolf struggling to pick up her apparently lifeless victim.

24

bee wolf fighting bee

Though the bee was almost as large as her attacker, the bee wolf had straddled her victim and was clasping it with her legs. When she launched herself into the air with her burden, her flight was so labored that it was a simple matter to follow close behind as she flew back toward the cliff less than twenty feet away.

The cliff slid down at a gentle angle for about fifteen to twenty feet before breaking up to form the rocky edge of a small, spring-fed stream. The loose, almost sandy soil that filled the crevices between the rough boulders on the side of the cliff was punctured with dozens of little burrows. Apparently each burrow belonged to a bee wolf because several of them were flying in low circles over the entrances. The one that had just returned with the bee was at first unable to decide which of the many burrows belonged to her. Several times she dropped her bee and nervously flitted about over the rocks, investigating each burrow until at last she seemed satisfied.

As the bee wolf came back for her bee, two tiny, parasitic flies buzzing nearby seemed to make her more nervous than ever. She darted into the air and flew at the pair, but they simply circled out of range until the wasp irritably returned to her bee. This time she took hold of it with her mandibles and roughly dragged it to a burrow in the shadow of one of the rocks.

At the entrance to her burrow the wolf grasped the bee's thorax with her legs and used her mandibles to bite its neck until a small drop of nectar was forced out of the bee's mouth. The little wolf greedily lapped it up and resumed her biting until she had squeezed all the nectar out of the bee's crop.

When the wolf was convinced that she had all the nectar, she left the bee lying there and disappeared into her burrow. After a minute or two she reappeared, again chased away the flies, then grabbed the bee with her mandibles. Turning around, she quickly backed into the narrow burrow with her victim. The disappointed flies took one last look as their prize disappeared; then they flew away in search of a less well-guarded bee on which to deposit their living maggots.

At least five minutes passed this time before the bee wolf reappeared. First she poked her twitching head just above the entrance and made a

26

quick survey of the surrounding territory. Seemingly satisfied, she crawled out and circled her burrow several times before flying away over the edge of the cliff.

What had she done with the bee? Since the bee wolf is known to live on nectar instead of fresh meat, she was not going to eat her victim. And she could have just as easily robbed it of its nectar at the point where she attacked it. Would she work that hard just to provide her victim with a decent funeral? The only way to find the answer would be to dig open the burrow even though the bee wolf wouldn't be too happy with me if she came back and found me tearing open her home and trying to steal her bee. Still, I was curious and foolish enough to take a chance on it.

As I worked my way over the edge of the cliff and found a projecting rock that would support me, I accidentally scraped away several smaller rocks and a clump of dried grass near the burrow. As long as the burrow itself wasn't damaged, this shouldn't have made any difference to the bee wolf. As a matter of fact it seemed to make quite a lot of difference.

The little wolf soon returned with another victim, but for some reason she dropped it so far away from her burrow that it rolled down the cliff and was lost. Seeming to ignore the loss of her bee, the bee wolf ran around in circles near where the ground had been disturbed by my climbing. She hopped up and down, made short flights, then ran in circles some more. She was becoming more excited every minute, even going so far as to run into her neighbors' burrows. They quickly showed her what they thought of that, and she came back out even faster than she had gone inside.

What was wrong with her? The burrow was just as she had left it. Not a grain of sand at the entrance itself had been disturbed. While I was puzzling over this mystery, another bee wolf returned to the vicinity of its own burrow a couple of feet away. Just as the first one had done earlier, the newcomer dropped its bee a short distance away and made several circles in the vicinity of its nest. Every once in awhile it would carefully examine a twig, a dried blade of grass, or a pebble half buried in the sand. As soon as this inspection was over, it would return to the dead bee and drag it straight to the burrow.

27

Could it be that the bee wolf memorizes the landmarks in her own neighborhood and locates her burrow by its position among these markers? That made sense. After all, human beings do the same thing. If a building contractor's wrecking crew made a mistake and accidentally tore up all the houses around yours, you might have a hard time believing that you were in the right neighborhood if you came home after the damage had been done.

Niko Tinbergen, a Dutch entomologist, discovered many years ago that the European bee wolf does use landmarks such as pebbles and twigs in order to find its own burrow. Using his approach to the problem, I set about to see if this also worked with American bee wolves. While my first bee wolf was still angrily trying to remember where she left her burrow, I carefully rearranged the pebbles and twigs lying near the other burrows in that area of the cliff. Within half an hour the air was full of angry and very frustrated bee wolves. At least half a dozen captured bees were lying around on the ground while their captors were trying to find their own burrows.

After awhile things began to calm down as almost all of the bee wolves eventually located their own burrows and dragged their bees out of sight. The first one refused to calm down however, and was soon making a worrisome nuisance of herself by buzzing around my ears. I finally had to clap her into a collecting bottle to keep her out of my way. The top had a wire screen cover so that she could breathe. There was no point in killing her just so that I could examine her nest.

Before I could begin excavating the burrow of my captive bee wolf, another interesting sight caught my attention. At least three females were coming and going from a single burrow. These fierce little wasps are not the least bit sociable, so this was a rare sight. What had apparently happened was that several of the young ones had hatched at about the same time and had still not left home.

While I watched, the sisters apparently had a quarrel that resulted in one of them leaving the burrow. The unhappy little wasp flew around the area for a few minutes, then alighted and began busily scraping out a new burrow not more than three inches away from the other one. Using her mandibles as well as her front pair of legs, she sent the dirt

28

bee wolves near burrows

flying for several inches. At this rate she soon disappeared below the surface of the ground. Every once in awhile she would back out and fly away as though tired of the whole thing. A few minutes later she would return to continue her digging. This would probably go on for several days before she was completely satisfied.

By this time it was early in the evening, and all the cliff-dwelling bee wolves were beginning to return home for the night. Two of the lazy males, who apparently had spent the day playing in the sunshine and drinking nectar from honeysuckle, soon returned to the vicinity of the females' burrows. They didn't seem to be at all bothered about the rearranged neighborhood because they planned to rough it anyway. They flew around for a brief time and then alighted on an undisturbed patch of ground. One of them spent a few minutes cleaning his antennae, but the other one quickly dug a shallow burrow in the loose soil. He had to stop several times and back out because the sand in that spot kept falling in on top of him. But at last he seemed to be satisfied with his temporary shelter. The other one finally crawled under a rock and went to sleep.

Now that things had quieted down somewhat, I took a pencil and a pair of forceps from my pocket and carefully opened the burrow in which I had originally been interested. The soil was so loose that the pencil had to be used to plug the burrow while the forceps were used to gently scrape away the top. When it appeared that the burrow might be as much as two feet long, I was finally forced to use a sharp stick to remove most of the soil above the burrow and then slowly work my way down to the pencil with the aid of the forceps. Fortunately the burrow ran back through a shallow pocket of soil between two rocks near the top of the cliff. If it had been dug under one of the rocks, it would have probably been impossible to locate the stored bees.

Before going much more than about twelve inches into the burrow, I accidentally dug into a roomy storage cell just to the side of the main burrow and connected to it by a small side tunnel. Inside the cell were the remains of what must have been at least half a dozen bees and one fat little bee wolf larva who was greedily devouring one of the last of the intact bees.

30

The little larva seemed to be almost full size, so the bees must have been in there for quite some time. Yet one of the last victims appeared to be still alive. Its antennae and legs were quivering so slightly that at first it appeared to be only the result of a slight breeze. I realized now what the bee wolves had been doing. Instead of killing their victims, they gave them a dose of poison that would only paralyze them. If they killed the bees, they might spoil before the larvae could finish them. In that case the larvae would starve to death.

It seemed such a gruesome fate for the bees that I was tempted to kill the fat, ugly larva. But this was only one small drama in the savage life of the insect jungles. It has been going on for millions of years and will no doubt continue for that many more. The bee wolves and the golden honeybees live but a short time. I didn't think that it was up to me to decide which should live the longer.

After carefully sheltering the exposed larva with a flat rock, I released the unhappy bee wolf from my collection jar. By now it was getting too dark to see, so I picked up my simple tools and quietly left the rocky cliff and the sleeping wolves. Tomorrow would bring its own adventures.

The Ant-Queen Kidnapper

My encounter with the bee wolves had reminded me of a discovery a month before of a ruthless band of kidnappers living in that same park. Their hideout was so carefully situated that it would have been quite difficult to find if I had not been able to watch one of them in the very act of kidnapping a real live queen! Even then it was not easy to follow the flight of the kidnapper with her victim because she was so much faster than the bee wolf.

This particular kidnapper was a determined little black wasp who was obviously new at the business of kidnapping anything. This may very well have been her first serious flight in search of living prey. The adults, like most wasps, live on nectar alone. When I came upon her while crossing the hard, dry ground of a baseball diamond in the park, she was flitting about a rather large nest of black ants. She would light

31

just to one side of the nest, run up to it, and then hop into the air when the angry workers swarmed out of the nest to do battle with her. Before the irritated ants could calm down, she would be back again making them even more angry than before.

Finally one of the bolder ants managed to grab the little kidnapper by one leg. Fortunately for the wasp the ant did not get a good hold, but the wasp whirled and thrashed about as she frantically tried to rid herself of the ant. It was one thing for the wasp to kidnap one of the ants, but it was quite another to have such an unwelcome hitchhiker hanging onto her leg.

The ant must have realized that she wasn't going to do much good chewing away on the wasp's leg because she either let go or let herself be shaken off. It would have been difficult to tell whether the wasp or the ant was more relieved by this.

But the dogged little wasp just would not give up. She danced and ran about, flitted back and forth over the nest, and occasionally seemed to be daring the ants to catch her. What on earth could she be after? She was too large to get inside the nest and certainly not foolish enough to try. But if she had wanted to kidnap any of these ants, she could easily have had her pick of the hundreds who were casting hungry looks at her. Was she playing some kind of foolhardy game? That seemed even more unlikely. Those who play games in the insect jungles soon end up as meat on another insect's table.

This dangerous sport went on for an hour or more before I finally saw what the stubborn wasp was waiting for. While the workers were busily defending their nest, a large queen ant with shining, transparent wings crawled out of the nest and into the hot sunlight. She seemed dazzled by the light at first, having spent all of her young life below the surface of the ground. But as she became accustomed to the glare, she took several steps forward, threw herself into the air, and promptly flew away without a single backward look. She was quickly followed by an ever-increasing number of other emerging queen ants until the ground seemed to be covered with them for several inches around the nest.

This was the moment for which the eager wasp had been waiting!

32

Selecting a queen almost under her feet, she pounced on top of it and drove her slender stinger into it so quickly that it was impossible to see where she had struck. The queen almost instantly went limp from the effects of the poison. Before the nearby workers could prevent it, the wasp grabbed the queen with her legs and lifted both of them into the air with her powerful wings.

The kidnapping took place so quickly that I would have missed it if I had blinked my eyes. I immediately stood up to see in which direction the wasp was moving, though it was obvious that she was going too fast for me to keep her in sight unless I got a move on. She led me on quite a chase over a distance of almost two hundred yards. Twice she seemed to disappear against the background of trees and underbrush at the far edge of the park. Each time I just kept going in the direction in which I had last seen her, and each time I was fortunate enough to catch a glimpse of her once again.

On the way I almost ran over a small group of picnickers. The wasp flew right over their heads, and I came very close to running right through their lunch. They gave me such a startled look that I knew it would hardly do to try to explain that I was chasing a wasp who had just kidnapped a queen ant.

Near the edge of the trees the tireless little kidnapper finally landed in a small, sandy clearing. She dropped her ant and then ran around the clearing searching for her burrow. There must have been thirty burrows in a circle less than ten feet in diameter, but she didn't pay the least attention to any of them. There was only one burrow in which she was interested. The only trouble was that she couldn't remember where she had left it.

Perhaps she had covered up the entrance to keep out thieves. Probably with this thought in mind she began scratching and pawing at the sand like an angry bull. She dug half a dozen shallow depressions before giving up and returning to her ant. For some reason she didn't have any problem finding her ant again. She picked it up with her legs, flicked her wings a couple of times, then apparently remembered where the burrow had been. She flew about three inches over to one side, dropped the ant, and ran into an empty burrow. A moment later she

33

aphilanthops and swarming black ant queens

popped back out and pulled the queen inside. While I waited for what must have been fifteen or twenty minutes, other kidnappers from the colony began bringing back queens of their own. It was not possible to know whether they were getting them from the same nest or not. But all the ants appeared to be the same species.

How do these wasps know the exact time at which the queen ants will emerge from a black ant nest? Though I have been unable to learn the answer to this puzzle, it is probable that they spend days examining the ant nests for emerging queens. Their instinct would somehow control the time of the year in which they begin their search, just as the instinct of the ants controls the time of the year in which their queens are readied for their flight.

After careful study of the ants that were being brought back to the kidnappers' hideout, it soon became evident that the victims were in various stages of paralysis. Some of them were almost completely unconscious, and a few may even have been dead. But it seemed that most of them were still alive and able to move to a limited extent. All still had their wings, which meant that they must have left their nests or had been dragged out of them this same day, because a queen ant loses her wings shortly after leaving the home nest.

Would the paralyzed ants recover? This seemed possible, but what would be the point in drugging a large number of queen ants just for the sake of kidnapping them without a struggle? For that matter, why kidnap them in the first place if the adult wasps live on nectar instead of fresh meat? You probably have guessed the answer now that you know what the bee wolves do with their captive bees. But at that time I had not yet discovered the bee wolves' secret; so I didn't know quite what to expect from the ant-queen kidnappers. As a matter of fact, things were a little different from what you would have expected, too.

For some reason that I cannot recall, I was carrying a gardener's trowel and some other unusual tools in my belt that day. It was a good thing, too, because the surface of the ground around the burrows was as hard as brick. And of course these little kidnappers like to dig their burrows as deep as possible. The harder the ground, the deeper the burrow—or at least that was the way it seemed under that hot July sun. By the time I had gone down about eight inches around one burrow, I came to a small cell that was practically stuffed with a clump of ants. Right in the middle of them was a tiny wasp larva who had apparently been hatched only a day or two before from an egg laid on one of the helpless ants.

It was in the second cell that I found a most unusual scene. I had dug down about another two or three inches when my trowel broke into a chamber that was stuffed with tiny white maggots of parasitic flies. Apparently one or more flies had laid their eggs or maggots, one or the other, on some of the captive ants. The kidnapper wouldn't have noticed this, but the larva would have. The fly maggots would have already eaten most of the ants by the time the wasp larva hatched from the egg. Sure enough, there was no wasp larva to be seen. Perhaps the maggots had even eaten the wasp egg. The mother wasp had gone to a lot of trouble to feed someone else's children. But then so had the ants who raised the young queens.

Hunting Guide

Scientific Names: (1) *Philanthus;* (2) *Aphilanthops.*

Common Names: *Philanthus* is commonly known as the bee wolf, though this name is borrowed from a European cousin that preys exclusively on honeybees.

Aphilanthops is commonly known as the ant-queen kidnapper, probably because this seems to be the only kind of work in which they show any real interest.

Description: *Philanthus* is about half an inch long. Its black and yellow body resembles that of a yellow jacket.

Aphilanthops is brownish-black with golden markings on its abdomen. The transparent wings are brownish. It is about one-fourth inch long.

bee wolf *(philanthus)*

36

Habitat: The **bee wolf** is most easily found on hot, clear days in August. In cool, cloudy weather they stay in the nest. They prefer to build their nests on sloping banks in the vicinity of flowers such as goldenrod and asters. Some other, smaller species may nest in either sloping or vertical banks, or even on flat ground.

The **kidnapper** is most commonly found early in July when it is busy biting and scratching in sandy soil as it begins its tunnel. The nest has a cup-shaped depression at the entrance, a place in which the ant may be dropped while the wasp enters the burrow. Two to three dozen nests may be built within a few feet of one another. Some of them may have the entrance blocked with soil or debris which serves as a door to keep out parasites. The wasps have a range of about one mile, so the nests may may not necessarily be near a source of the black ants on which they prey.

Stalking Methods: A search for the bee wolf should be made in fields or gardens frequented by wild honeybees and by the much smaller wild bees described in Chapter 6. The more flowers and bees, the greater the chance of finding the bee wolves. Look for their nests around the steep banks of drainage ditches and dirt or gravel roads. They are most common in August during clear, hot weather.

The ant-queen kidnapper is most easily found early in July in dry, sandy areas only sparsely covered with grass and weeds. The nests will probably be more common in an area in which nests of the black ants may also be found.

kidnapper wasp carrying
ant queen to nest

4
The Slave Hunters

You have probably watched many a fierce battle between armies of television actors and extras dressed as anything from medieval knights to modern soldiers. But the first time that you actually see this happening in a vacant lot or city park near your home, television will never be the same again. If I told you right away that I was talking about ants instead of human warriors, you might just go turn your television set on again. At least that was the way that I felt until the day that I saw the bloodred slave hunters in action.

One day early in July an enthusiastic insect-hunting friend of mine told me about a colony of slave-hunting Amazon ants in a small park near my home. At first I thought he was joking. Who ever heard of slave-hunting ants? By the time he was finally able to convince me that he was telling the truth, he was too irritated to tell me where in the park I could find them. Nevertheless, this was something that I had to see for myself.

The park didn't seem so small after all when I tried to track down a single colony of ants, but I finally found them after a month of searching. Then it took three more weeks of daily observation of the elusive Amazons to catch them launching an attack on a distant village of smaller black ants. But there was enough adventure in that one afternoon to last for years to come.

Though the Amazons were almost half an inch long, their small scouting parties were too skillful to attract much attention as they carefully searched the tangled grassland jungles of the park. Some of these scouts would make trips over a distance of several hundred yards, while a few of the lazier ones seemed content to explore their own backyard.

The nest that I found was a large one that probably contained two or three thousand warriors and almost as many slaves. The small black slaves went out in daily search of food, and it was they who formed the familiar winding trail to a crust of bread or to the body of a dead beetle. Most of the warriors seemed to prefer staying indoors while the little captives did all the work.

Finally, on a hot and dusty afternoon I found a small group of scouts running back toward the nest with a show of great excitement. As I sometimes did on trips in search of colonies of insects, I was carrying a small bottle of bright orange paint with which to mark some individuals from the colony. The scouts had taken me by surprise, though, and I barely had time to daub a speck of paint on the abdomen of one sleepy red warrior drowsing in the sunlight at the edge of the nest.

At the touch of the tiny brush in my hand, the little warrior jumped straight up and then darted into the smooth walled tunnel entrance of her home. The scouts poured into the hole almost on her heels as they eagerly searched for other warriors to whom they could make their report. Several seconds passed; then the orange-spotted Amazon peered cautiously above the rim of the nest. Moments later the darkness behind her erupted with what must have been for the ants a deafening chorus of squeals and the clattering of thousands of running feet. Before the startled Amazon could get out of the way, a swarming mass of her sister warriors almost trampled her as they darted upwards in a mad dash for the nest entrance.

The unhappy orange-spotted ant, whom I decided to call Agilla, had no choice but to be among the first of the Amazons boiling out of the main entrance into the sun-sprinkled shadows. A shaft of sunlight filtered down through the towering grassblade trees and flashed from her polished red armor as she pushed her way through the scrambling horde. Within minutes the Amazons had formed a long column, and the forward elements were already marching off into the surrounding weed jungle before the last of the warriors spewed forth from the darkness of the main tunnel.

Once the march was well underway, Agilla was probably able to learn that she was part of an invasion force preparing to make a surprise

39

attack on a small colony of black ants. During the past winter the number of slaves in the Amazon nest most likely had been greatly reduced through disease and hunting accidents. In this case, the existence of the colony was now in grave danger unless new slaves could be found. Vicious fighters that they are, the Amazons have no equals in courage and ability to make war. Yet they are completely unable to feed themselves or to care for their own young. Their mighty jaws are so specialized for warfare that they have lost the ability to do any useful work. If they did not have slaves to feed them, they would soon starve to death.

The trail that the red warriors followed wound through the shadowy coolness of the jungle, around deep lakes formed by a recent rainstorm, and across the shifting sand dunes of a baseball diamond desert.

The trip across the desert was one of the most dangerous parts of the entire invasion march. Here the cone-shaped pits of the ant lions claimed the lives of two of the more careless warriors. They passed too close to the shifting sands at the edges of the pits and had suddenly dropped out of sight of the column never to be seen again.

There was also the ever-present danger that windblown dust would cover the scent trail left by the returning scouts. Fortunately the more experienced old leaders were able to pick up the ends of a broken trail before the other warriors could be thrown into confusion.

As the marchers left the desert and entered the jungle on the opposite side, some of the scouts climbed to the very top of the gently swaying grassblade trees. After waving their antennae about to pick up the mixture of odors drifting from the nearby black ant colony, they would scurry down the other side and eagerly rejoin the marchers.

By the time the approach to the objective had begun, almost all the warriors were snapping their jaws and increasing their pace. All but the lazy Agilla! She was not only tired after a two-hundred yard march, but she was also very likely to be getting hungry again. Needless to say, she was in a terrible humor. But true warrior that she was, she was among the first of the reckless warriors that hurled themselves boldly into the attack. Perhaps she felt that the sooner the battle was over the sooner she would eat again.

40

Amazon ants, scouts

The startled black ant workers had been so busy carving up the still fresh body of a field cricket that the attackers were almost upon them before their scouts flashed a warning along the ranks of the food-bearing column. Just for a moment the workers were swept with uncertainty and confusion; then they dropped their cricket hamburgers and swarmed back to defend their besieged nest. By the time the first of the Amazons had reached the entrance of the nest, the defenders had buried them in the first wave of the counterattack.

Agilla quickly found herself at the center of a rolling black ball of clawing feet and snapping jaws. The furious little defenders clung to her antennae, to her legs, and even to the joints of her armor. Half a dozen pairs of slashing jaws ripped scars along her tough body. Others chewed on her legs or tried to tear off her antennae while spraying formic acid in her face. Agilla was doing quite a lot of damage herself. Her powerful jaws were tearing and slashing with deadly effect, but still it seemed that she would soon be completely overcome. She was not alone in her desperate battle. All around her the other Amazons were fighting desperately for their lives while some of the black ant workers scurried inside their nest and began sealing the entrance against the attackers.

Then even as Agilla went down, the bulk of the attackers reached the nest and began tearing the maddened defenders from her injured body. As the last of her tormentors was pulled off and tossed aside, Agilla rose somewhat shakily to her feet and charged back into the battle.

By now the reinforcements had broken up the ranks of the defenders and were steadily driving them back into the jungle's edge. The uninjured latecomers busied themselves with tearing apart the sealed nest entrance. As soon as the hole was large enough to admit them, they darted inside to clear out the last of the defenders. For several minutes solitary battles continued; then all was quiet.

The surviving Amazons who were not too crippled to walk made their way into the nest. Soon afterwards they reappeared with squirming bundles of white clamped gently but firmly in their jaws. These were the first of the helpless larvae and pupae that would be carried

42

back to the Amazon nurseries as the spoils of war. Once safely placed in the Amazon nurseries, they would be reared as slaves for the colony.

The ground was literally covered with bodies by the time the last battle had ended. Here and there a badly injured warrior tried without success to drag herself back to her comrades as they marched off into

Amazon ants with grubs

the jungle with their captives. It was of no use. Not one marcher turned back to help. The dying fighters were of no use to either colony.

As the victorious warriors emerged from the darkness of the jungle at the edge of their nest, they were met by a welcoming committee of slaves who immediately took charge of both warriors and captives. As soon as the last of the new larvae and pupae were safely stored in the nurseries, the slaves would turn to cleaning and feeding their weary masters. I noticed that the exhausted Agilla was given a drop of honey as soon as she dragged herself to the edge of the nest. Then several of the slaves came out and led her inside to clean her wounds. By the next day she would probably be out sunning herself again.

The action outside the nest was over for now, but parasitic beetles living deep within the nest would soon be busy laying their own eggs among the new supply of larvae and pupae which would serve as food for the beetle larvae. These interesting pests are not only tolerated; they are even encouraged to stay in the safety of the nest. The Amazons ignore them, but the slaves like them because they have tiny, honey-producing hairs on their backs. Whenever a slave comes upon one of them, she always stops to milk a drop or two of honey from the hairs.

Milking the parasitic beetles is not among the slaves' regular duties. They must enlarge the nest when necessary, keep the caverns clean, raise the young of both species, and even keep their masters clean and well fed. They could refuse to feed the Amazons, and soon there would be no Amazons left. Unfortunately, there would soon be no slaves left in the Amazon nest, either. Without a queen, the colony would gradually die out and might even perish under an attack by a stronger tribe of black ants seeking new territory. Of course such an attack would never succeed when the lazy but war-loving Amazons are at home.

A nest of Amazons may be as much as fifteen years old, but is more likely to be only two or three years old. Early each spring when the ground has begun to warm up enough, the slaves clean and feed a newly hatched group of winged males and females who will soon leave the nest and fly away to attempt to start new colonies. Both males and young queens may fly for several miles, the queens searching for a suitable nesting location and the males searching for queens from

44

other nests. Only a small number of males will ever mate, and these soon afterward die of hunger and exhaustion after their long trip. Most of the females will meet the same fate unless they are fortunate enough to locate a young or weak nest of black ants. Once the queen has found a home, her wings will either fall off, or she will rub them off before she settles down for a period of as much as fifteen years of constant egg laying.

When the Amazon queen is taken to the royal egg-producing chamber, she will find that a black ant queen is already making herself quite comfortable there. The Amazon queen will generously tolerate this for several days before turning around and biting the head off the other queen. Her unknowing slaves will soon remove the useless body of their dead mother and toss it out of the nest. There are no feelings of love or sympathy in the ant colony.

As the first Amazon eggs are laid, the workers obediently carry them off to the nursery and watch over them until the wormlike white larvae hatch from the eggs. These helpless little grubs are fed with droplets of honey or mashed insects prepared and stored in the crops of the nursery workers, then regurgitated at feeding time. The larvae grow quickly on this rich diet and soon reach the point at which they form a sort of cocoon about themselves and go into the resting or pupal stage. When it comes time for them to break out of their soft covering, the nurses help tear it open and assist the young ant as she struggles to stand up on still unsteady legs. The fact that they are suddenly beginning to pull out big red ants instead of small black ones apparently never bothers them. An ant is an ant to them. These newly emerged adults are weak and unsteady at first, but as the workers clean and feed them, they quickly grow stronger and their soft skin begins to harden and turn darker.

It is the habit of a well-fed ant to share food from her crop with hungry fellow workers; so it would seem only natural that they do not hesitate to keep the lazy Amazons well fed. The busy workers have no way of knowing that the hungry Amazon is not doing her part in getting food for the rest of the colony.

When the original supply of black ants begins to be reduced in number for lack of a queen of their own, the new Amazon colony must send out scouts to find a new supply of workers. If they fail, the colony will one day be only a network of empty caverns with perhaps the lonely, shriveled body of the Amazon queen lying somewhere in the darkness below.

Hunting Guide

Scientific Names: (1) *Polyergus;* (2) *Formica.*

Common Names: *Polyergus* is commonly known as the Amazon ant or as the robber ant.

The slave-hunting species of *Formica* is called the sanguinary ant, the bloodred ant, or the slave-making ant.

The slaves belong to the genus *Formica.*

Description: These two different species are similar in appearance and in slave-making habits, but the **Amazon ant** is completely dependent upon its slaves, while the **sanguinary ant** uses them only as assistants in the care of their colony.

The warrior-workers of both species are about three-eighths inch long. Both have the huge, saberlike jaws so effective in battle. The head of the Amazon ant is smaller and more oval shaped than the somewhat heart-shaped head of the sanguinary ant. Both species have a slender thorax attached by a characteristically thin stalk to the oval-shaped abdomen. The color ranges from a distinctive red to a duller brownish-red. Sanguinary workers may have a brown or black abdomen. The bulbous abdomen of both species is made up of four rather clearly marked segments.

Amazon ant *(polyergus)*

46

Habitat: Both species are found primarily in the eastern part of the United States. The nest of the Amazon ant is always the same as that of the little gray or black ants who serve them. No wonder, since the Amazon queen who started the colony did so in an appropriated black ant nest!

The sanguinary ants often build their nests in old stumps or logs. When they build underground nests, they would be entirely below the surface, and not built partially in a mound of soil.

Stalking Methods: If you can find an area in which the nests of black or gray ants are numerous, you will be likely to find the scouts of one of the two species of slave hunters. It is possible that you will even locate a former black ant nest now occupied by the Amazons. After a scout has been located, you may have to follow her for several hours before she leads you in the direction of the nest which could be two or three hundred yards away.

formica

If the nests of the black ants are not easily found, try putting out sugar or honey bait at intervals of fifty or one hundred feet. Check these daily for the appearance of columns of ants taking the food back to their hidden nests.

Slave making expeditions usually start out in the early afternoon during the hot summer months. You would probably be wasting your time if you watch for them in early spring or late in the fall. But then you never know!

Check the vicinity of old logs and stumps for sanguinary workers and scouts.

an old stump, favorite haunt of sanguinary workers and scouts

47

5

The Terrible Falcons
of the Grassland

The Spider Hunters

Anyone who is familiar with the ancient art of falconry is well aware that the European peregrine falcon is considered to be the noblest representative of all the distinguished clan of falcons. The master falconer is equally well aware that some of the peregrine's kinfolk can occasionally be somewhat less than noble, especially when they are hungry. Out on the dry Kansas prairie you may sometimes be able to see scattered puffs of dust raised by a pigeon hawk as she repeatedly misses her young jackrabbit prey. The fact that she keeps diving into the ground doesn't seem to bother her at all. She just bounces back into the air and tries again. Now if this sounds ridiculously awkward, wait until you see some of the insect falcons hunting their prey. Some of them have made an art of using the most ridiculous hunting methods possible.

One of the most excitable and clumsy of all the insect falcons is a little black and orange spider-hunting wasp. The first one that I ever met was so busy fighting with a wolf spider in my backyard that she didn't have any time to worry about me. When I first spotted them, the hairy gray spider was reared up against a rotting stump that was successfully interfering with the little wasp's tactics. The wasp, only half an inch long, seemed hardly a match for the fangs of this fearsome spider, a fact that seemed also to cause her just a little concern. She was twitching her wings, waving her antennae, and leaping up and down in front of the spider as though her nerves were about to explode. The harder she bounced and twitched, the more nervous the spider became. Finally she made her grand move and leaped onto the spider's back. He just as promptly bucked her off and leaped toward her as

48

she tried to bounce out of his way. His dripping fangs gnashed together just beneath her feet as she sprang into the air and again dropped onto his back. When he bucked her off this time, she really came apart at the seams. She bounced around and flew back and forth over the confused and angry spider until he must have been too dizzy to get out of her way when she leaped on top of him the third time. This time her stinger plunged into him in a twinkling of a second, and he collapsed almost instantly.

Now the little wasp could relax and catch her breath. But instead of relaxing, she climbed down from her paralyzed prey and came around to the front of him. There she peered at his fangs with great curiosity. Suddenly she darted around and grabbed one of the huge legs in her mandibles, giving it such a mighty tug that the spider almost rolled over on top of her. She just as suddenly released it and again ran around to the front to examine its fangs as though to be quite certain that the spider was really helpless. She was almost touching the fangs when the spider twitched convulsively. The startled little wasp shot straight up into the air and circled her victim twice before daring to alight again.

At last the wasp seemed satisfied that all was well. She carefully grabbed one of the spider's legs and backed off into the grass with him. Three or four feet away she laboriously backed up the trunk of a young maple tree, dragging her burden along with great difficulty. She climbed several feet high and then leaped off into space with what was probably intended to be a graceful dive. Instead, she plummeted down at a sharp angle—in the same direction from which she had just come with such an effort.

Just above the ground she dropped her spider. The paralyzed creature bounced once as he hit the ground, then fell back in a crumpled heap. The irritated wasp must have felt that her troubles were all the fault of the helpless spider because she pounced on him and began furiously hacking away at his legs with her sharp mandibles. By the time she chewed off two of his legs, she had calmed down to her former nervous self.

Now the little wasp apparently decided that it was time to hide her prey from possible thieves. Ignoring her mangled spider for a brief

49

spider-hunting wasp dragging wolf spider up maple

period, she half ran and half flew through the grass, stopping every once in awhile to investigate a burrow or crack in the dry ground. At the base of a wild sunflower at the edge of the back fence, she found a shallow hole in the ground. This seemed to satisfy her. She now took to the air and flew back across the grass to the spot where she had left her spider.

As soon as the wasp reached her spider, she saw at once that her worst fears had been realized. Her prey was being dragged off by three big black carpenter ants. She leaped at the ants as though she would tear them apart; yet she was smart enough not to land within reach of them. Fortunately her sudden rush seemed to upset the hungry thieves, and they fled without offering any resistance.

The wasp bounced up and down with apparent pleasure at her great victory. Then she chewed off another spider leg for luck before dragging the body off toward the sunflower. This time she stayed on the ground and ignored the maple tree. By the time she neared the sunflower, she seemed to have forgotten where she had left the shallow hole. After fifteen or twenty minutes of frantic searching, she finally found it. She spent quite some time now digging a burrow deeper into the ground, using the shallow hole as an entrance to the more narrow burrow that she was preparing.

When the burrow was completed to her satisfaction, the little wasp flew back to her spider and wearily dragged it to the entrance. It went into the entrance without any trouble, but was too fat to fit into the burrow. This was just too much for the weary, bedraggled wasp. She leaped onto the spider and bounced up and down on it repeatedly, stopping only long enough to chew on its remaining legs. She alternated between bouncing and chewing for ten or fifteen minutes during which it seemed that she would surely collapse from nervous exhaustion. But finally she managed to wear the spider down to the proper size so that she could drag it back into the burrow with only a small amount of effort.

Half an hour went by without a sign of the wasp, and I thought that she had probably blocked herself when she dragged the spider down behind her. There was so little room there that I was sure the spider would make an airtight plug. But she fooled me. She darted out of the burrow so unexpectedly that I barely managed to get my nose out of her way. After covering the entrance with bits of leaves and dried grass, she paused to clean her antennae and to scratch at her mandibles with one of her front legs. Then she took to the air and disappeared across the back fence.

Later on in the day I saw what was probably the same little wasp with a smaller spider dangling from her mandibles. She was flying back into the tangled jungle of a flower bed full of tall blue bachelor's buttons. She probably buried this little spider just as she had the first one.

This spider-hunting wasp lives on the nectar of flowers and she has no use for spider steaks—no matter how delicious they might be. However, her larvae enjoy nothing more than a luncheon of tasty wolf spider. There really isn't much to do but eat in a tiny earthen cell several inches below the surface of the ground.

Though I do sometimes dig up the burrows of the hunting wasps in an effort to learn more about them, I just didn't have the heart to bother a burrow that was built and stocked with such effort. Besides, I already knew quite a lot about this particular species of wasp. First she would lay an egg on the spider, and the egg would hatch in two or three days. The larva that hatched from it would spend two weeks feasting on the spider (which may be the reason that adults are vegetarians).

When the two weeks had passed, the larva would spin a cocoon about herself and then spend the coming winter within the silken envelope. When she had passed through the pupal stage the following spring, the now hardened cocoon would split open and the young hunting wasp would emerge to begin a life of her own.

If this little wasp survived, she would spend the summer feeding on the flowers in her hunting territory. In the fall she would mate and would then begin her own spider hunting.

Unfortunately for the young wasp, my curiosity overcame me by the following spring, and I dug up the burrow after all. Sure enough, the helpless pupa was indeed lying there in her hardened cocoon just as I had expected. She had survived every hazard of life in the soil when

I carefully transported her to the shelter and security of a terrarium. When the little pupa died a few days later, I was sorry to lose her, remembering the frantic activities of her mother to provide for her.

The Cement Makers

If you were on the way to your nearest supermarket, and a near-sighted rattlesnake challenged you, would you defend yourself with only a pocketknife? Not very likely! But when a grocery-shopping mud dauber wasp stumbles across the even more fearsome black widow spider, she does not hesitate to match her own slender dagger against her enemy's often poisonous fangs. It is different for these slender-bodied little falcons, though, because for them the black widow *is* the supermarket.

While hunting scorpions in an abandoned pasture near a swamp in Louisiana, I witnessed a very spectacular attack by these steel-blue falcons. It was also an extremely fortunate attack as far as I was concerned, because I had stepped almost into the middle of a large number of black widows. In an abandoned pasture I had found a rotting rowboat lying upside down and about hidden by spiny thistles and flowering orchard grass. It was an unlikely spot for a rowboat, but an ideal situation for scorpions. But when I turned the boat over and stepped on the ground that it had been covering, black widow spiders began scurrying in every direction over the moldy ground. Their dozens of webs almost covered the inside of the boat. There must have been enough poison running around there to kill at least two mules and one scorpion hunter.

Before I could jump back, two hunting mud daubers buzzed past my ears, peeled off, then dived into the middle of the running spiders like miniature dive bombers. One straddled a huge black widow that had been running across my shoe. Before the frightened spider could turn to defend herself, the wasp had driven her stinger into the soft belly of the spider. The paralyzed black widow folded up almost instantly. A moment later the little falcon lifted her prey and flew back toward the nearby swamp, carrying the helpless spider with her legs.

53

mud dauber and black widow spider (orchard grass)

The second wasp missed her first target, but wheeled and grabbed another spider that had lunged blindly in her direction. As she took off with her victim, I realized with horror that she had forgotten to use her stinger. When the flailing legs of the equally horrified spider struck the abdomen of the wasp, she methodically curled her abdomen under the spider and drove her stinger into it. That was the end of that.

As I whirled about to follow the second mud dauber wasp, a third one dived into the middle of the spiders. I would never know if she made a capture, because I wanted to keep the other little falcon in sight.

Running across the overgrown pasture turned out to be quite an adventure in itself. Although there were no picnickers to run over, I did manage to step on the tail of a spotted skunk who had been sleeping in a small brush pile in my path. With a horrible screech he bounded into the air and came down running—right behind me. Looking back at it now, I think the black widows were much less frightening than that infuriated skunk galloping along on my heels. Fortunately he gave up the chase before I reached the swamp, or I would really have been in trouble. The briars and weeds in the swamp were just too thick for me to be able to run through them.

By the time I reached the moss-draped cypress trees at the swamp's edge, I wasn't the least worried about quicksand or water moccasins. Anyone who has just stepped on the tail of a full-grown skunk isn't inclined to worry about little things like that. The only thing that did worry me was that I seemed to have lost my two mud daubers. I knew that they would not have gone too far, though. The nests had probably been built in some sheltered spot nearby, most likely in a hollow log or under the branches of a fallen tree.

After half an hour of fruitless searching, I finally came upon an old weatherbeaten shack that leaned awkwardly to one side. It looked abandoned, but you just don't come up on a house in the swamp without warning any possible inhabitants. Some of the swamp dwellers didn't mind spider webs built across empty windows, but they did mind strangers. When several loud calls failed to produce a rifle barrel in a window, or even a squeaking board, I carefully circled the shack before walking across the front door, long since off its hinges.

To my surprise and delight the abandoned shack proved to be the home of several dozen blue and yellow mud daubers who were busily coming and going through one of the windows. Every corner of the musty front room was stuffed with the cylindrical mud cells that the wasps must have been building for several years.

While I was looking over the cells in one corner, a mud dauber arrived at one cell that was still open at one end. She hummed contentedly to herself as she alighted on the wall with a large gray spider and quickly stuffed it into the cell. As soon as she had tucked it inside, she flew off again. Other wasps in the room were doing exactly the same thing. They would bring in spiders of practically every description and stuff their cells with them. Others were building new nests with little balls of mud that they brought in from the slippery banks of a nearby bayou.

I should have noticed that it was suddenly getting much darker outside, but I had been too busy watching the wasps to notice an ominous change in the weather. The fascinating little wasps never worked together. Some would be hunting while others were spending their time building new cells. A mud dauber would bring in a little ball of mud which she would pat into shape at the open end of her partially completed cell. She would make a part of a ring with one load and would complete it with a second load. Each ring would add a little to the length of the cell until finally only a small opening remained at one end. Additional loads of mud would be spread over the outside of the rings to add strength to the entire cell. From the number of rings that made up one cell, I could tell that it must have taken forty to fifty loads of mud for each one. Then each cell had to be stuffed with spiders. Curious to see the interior of the storage cells and their contents, I broke into several of them. The first two sealed cells contained nothing at all but spiders. The third one had apparently been built by a forgetful wasp, because it was empty. It was the fourth cell that held the answer for which I had been searching. A long, white wasp larva was happily munching on one of the spiders sharing her crowded cell. Or at least she apparently had been enjoying her meal before I broke open the cell and she and her paralyzed guests fell to the floor.

The shack was so dark by now that it was getting difficult to see anything more; so I decided to leave before the gathering storm broke. Before I could take a step toward the door, a tremendous burst of lightning seemed to explode right outside the door. By the light of that flash I saw the spotted skunk running into the shack to take shelter from the thunderstorm. By the time the skunk had crossed the front door, I was already out the window and running back toward the pasture. From that day on I never bothered another mud dauber.

The Paper House Builders

Like the rogue elephants that destroy the crops of villagers in some parts of India, some of the ordinarily helpful creatures of the insect jungles can at times be both dangerous and destructive. One of the most unpredictable and dangerous of all is a small red wasp commonly known as the paper house builder. These inch-long creatures haven't been welcome around my home since I briefly shared a hiding place with them twenty years ago.

Some of my friends and I had been playing hide-and-go-seek on my grandmother's farm. I had chosen a large concrete drainpipe that ran under a gravel road, a hiding place that had never been used by any of the other boys. I carefully backed into the pipe without bothering to inspect it first. That was my first mistake. My second mistake was in not moving fast enough when I heard the ominous buzzing sound just over my head. When I turned to see what was making the sound, I found myself staring into the shining black eyes of what must have been two dozen red wasps. Every one of them seemed to be poised with her wings spread ready for an attack.

If you have ever seen a man shot from a cannon at a circus, you will have a good idea of how I looked coming out of that drainpipe. I headed straight for a small herd of big-boned red mules gathered near the gravel road. They scattered in every direction as the wasps and I went through them. The hooves of the excited mules were flying so close as they lashed out with their hind legs that I could feel the breeze from them whooshing past my head. This distracted the wasps who quit following me and took out after the mules. When I fell to

57

the ground to catch my breath, I could see angry mules running everywhere—sometimes taking fences with them.

As the years passed and I became better acquainted with the life stories of insects, I realized that even the red wasps are usually harmless as long as their nest isn't being threatened. Just be sure to notice that I said usually and not always. One day I was out working on my front lawn when two red wasps dive-bombed me just because I was walking beneath a nest that was at least twenty feet up in a redbud tree.

Five minutes later I was halfway up that tree with a pressurized can of insect spray. The only thing that saved the nest was my curiosity when I noticed that one of the wasps was carrying back what appeared to be a short, fat caterpillar. She alighted on the edge of the nest, then started chewing the caterpillar into a ball of meat. A few minutes later she was busily stuffing the chopped meat into the open cells in which I could see brownish-white heads of wasp larvae.

The can of insect spray was forgotten as I balanced in a crotch of the tree and watched the wasps. Not every one of them was bringing back meat for the young. Some were bringing back muddy-white balls of wood pulp or well-chewed shreds of newspaper which they gradually built onto the nest. The cells in the center of the nest were obviously deeper than those around the edges, though larvae of different sizes seemed to be growing in about a third of the open cells regardless of their depth. Another third of the cells were capped with a thin sheet of paper, and the remainder were open and apparently empty for the moment.

There was one wasp somewhat larger and fatter than the others. She did not leave the nest a single time while I remained in the tree. Instead of making flights for wood pulp or for food for the young, she was busily laying eggs in the empty cells. If one of the other females laid an egg in one of the cells, the larger wasp would find it and destroy it so that she could lay her own egg in its place.

After awhile two of the bolder workers foolishly attacked me, but were easily discouraged by a cloud of insecticide. The remaining workers had provided me with so much interesting knowledge of the life of the red wasps that I decided to leave the nest intact for the rest

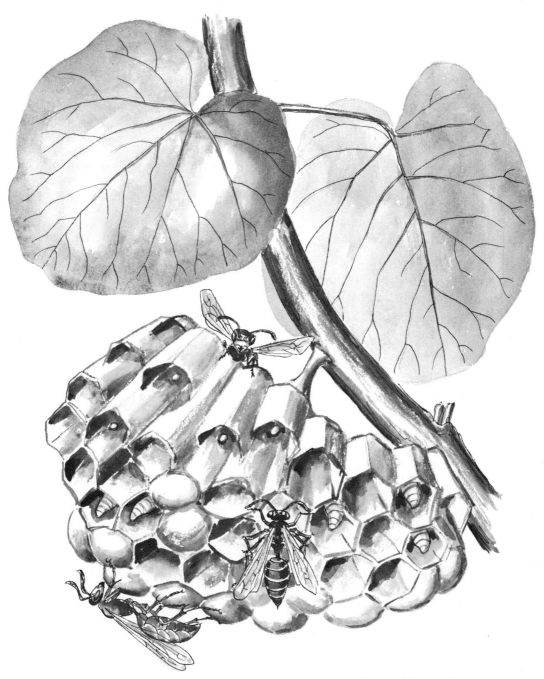

paper wasps on nest (California redbud)

of the year. By the onset of the cool weather of autumn, the nest had grown in size until it was almost eight inches across. Since many if not most of the cells would have been used several times that season, it was probable that three or four hundred wasps had been hatched from that one nest. Yet there didn't seem to be any one time when there were more than two or three dozen wasps on the nest. It seemed unlikely that they were lost in combat for they have few natural enemies. Where did they all go?

During this same year I had collected several hot-tempered workers from that nest when they made the mistake of attacking me. While checking through my collection at the end of the summer, I noticed that the hatching wasps gradually became larger as the season progressed. Apparently the workers hatched early in the spring are smaller than those from later hatchings because of the scarcity of food in late spring and early summer. All but the fat queen probably live only for several weeks and would be replaced by those hatched later in the year. Thus there would be several generations of increasingly larger workers hatched out throughout the summer. The egg-laying female, who is also queen of the nest, would be larger than the workers because she hatched out late in the previous year when game was easily found.

As the time for the first frost approached, some of the larger wasps began leaving the nest one at a time and never returned. These were the young queens who would mate with the few smaller males emerging at about the same time. Soon the smaller males would drift away and die a lonely death while the fertilized young queens would seek out hiding places in which to hibernate during the coming winter.

Each day the weather became cooler, and each day the remaining workers would grow less active and would often spend hours clinging to the almost abandoned nest. And then one day a cold wind came down out of the northwest, bringing a touch of frost with it. One by one the lonely workers folded their wings in the chill wind and fell from the nest. By morning the nest was only an empty shell—a monument to better times.

In some sheltered spot such as the attic of a house or beneath the bark of a dying tree the queens would now be sleeping while new life lay dormant within their bodies. They would awaken the following spring, and life would begin again at some new nest site. There would be no time then to remember the faithful workers of seasons past.

Hunting Guide

Scientific Names: (1) *Pompilus;* (2) *Sceliphron;* (3) *Polistes.*

Common Names: *Pompilus* is one of a large group of hunting wasps that may be called simply hunting wasps or spider hunters.

Sceliphron is known as the mud dauber, dirtdobber, mason, or mason wasp.

Polistes may be known as the wasp, red wasp, or paper-making wasp.

Description: *Pompilus* is half an inch long. It is black with a reddish-orange waistband.

Sceliphron is a dull black wasp with yellow markings on the base of the antennae, on the legs, and on the thorax and abdomen. Sunlight flashing from her black armor sometimes gives it a steel-blue sheen similar to that of a species of mud dauber wasp other than the one described in this chapter. The adult is about one inch long, with about a third of its length being made up of a threadlike waist.

Polistes varies in color from dark red to brown and brownish-black. The adult is almost an inch long.

Habitat: All three of these insect falcons may be found feeding on nectar of various flowers by early summer. Except for *Polistes,* they will not begin taking live prey until late in the summer when it comes time for them to lay their eggs. The spider hunters fly on sunlit days. They

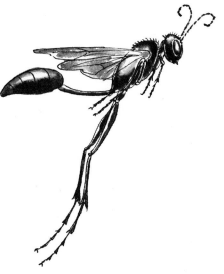

mud dauber in flight

paper wasp *(polistes)*

refuse to leave home if the sun is covered by clouds. The mud daubers and red wasps are not so particular.

The **spider hunters** may be found flying just above the ground in almost any weed-filled or brushy area in which ground spiders are readily found. They investigate cracks in the ground, spaces under porch steps, and piles of rock or brush in which the night-hunting spiders may be sleeping.

The **mud daubers** may be found gathering mud at the edge of almost any pond or drainage ditch. Their nests may be found in abandoned buildings, under bridges, or even on the ceiling of old porches.

The **red wasps** may be found around flower and vegetable gardens where they do their hunting, and on old rotted logs or around rotting newspapers from which they obtain the pulp for their nests. They build the grayish-white nests in thick brush, under the eaves of houses, in trees, and in shrubbery next to houses.

Stalking Methods: Look for all three wasps feeding on wild flowers as well as on cultivated flowers. The spider hunters will not be making their search for spiders until late in the summer.

mud dauber nest

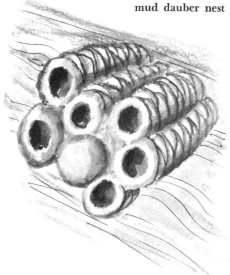

Look for mud daubers around pools of water and in places where they would be likely to build their nests. They may also be found searching for spiders in buildings such as a barn or an old garage.

The red wasps and their darker colored relatives may be found most easily in shrubbery around houses, or building their nests under the eaves of houses.

6
The Cave Dwellers

The Mysterious Solitary Bee

Probably in all the African forests and Indian jungles there are fewer than a dozen species of wild mammals about which modern biologists have little information. Yet in the insect jungles of the United States alone there are untold thousands of species of wild creatures about which almost nothing is known. Among the cave-dwelling bees alone there are almost five thousand species about which no published information is available. Does this sound impossible? Well, the chances are that there are several dozen different species of wild bees living off the wild flowers and flower gardens in your neighborhood. Have you ever seen any of them? Honeybees don't count, since they are not native wild bees.

If there are dandelions blooming in your neighborhood right now, find a patch of them and wait there for a few minutes. Do you see the miniature honeybees alighting on them after you become still? They are mostly little fellows, not more than one-fourth inch long. Some of them are little over one-eighth inch long. Most of them will be black with red, yellow, or greenish-metallic markings. If you have never noticed them before, it is probably only because you never realized that they existed. When you begin making a careful examination of individual flowers and empty looking patches of grass, you will discover some creatures so rare that they do not even have a name.

Why is there so little known about the wild bees? Are they so unimportant that there is no need to bother with them? As a matter of fact they are some of the most important insects in the United States. Several hundred different species play an important part in the pollination of cultivated crops; yet biologists do not even know where many of these wild bees build their lone nests. Perhaps your own safaris will held to add to the present meager store of knowledge about these unusual little creatures.

If you were surprised that you had never seen any of these miniature bees before, you will know exactly how I felt several years ago when I discovered them for the first time only after reading about them in a book. Fifteen minutes later I was finding wild bees all over my backyard. They were enjoying my unwelcome crop of dandelions far more than I did.

The bees in my backyard were the well-known sweat bees that are readily attracted to perspiring hands. They will occasionally alight and give you a painful sting for no reason at all. A British entomologist once wrote that they had such feeble stings that they could not penetrate human skin. But don't pick one up with your bare hands the way I did. This man wasn't talking about American sweat bees!

Of course I was curious to know more about the little sweat bees once I knew that they existed. But how do you go about following them home when you can hardly see them even while they are sitting still? The best course of action seemed to be an extended scouting expedition in a likely nesting territory. Since sweat bees like wide open spaces and dry, sandy soil, it didn't seem too likely that they would be nesting in my neighborhood. There were too many shade trees and well-watered lawns to suit the sweat bees. They prefer sunbaked soil that is well packed because poorly drained soil and rich humus encourage the growth of various molds that would destroy the eggs and the bee larvae. These bees have enough problems without that.

Fortunately the best and most likely hunting territory near my home was the city park in which I had found many different species of insects in the past several years. Though it was not an unusually large park, it was big enough to have almost all kinds of insect nesting sites within its borders. I knew that these so-called solitary bees sometimes cover several acres of ground with their burrows arranged in a sort of colony, though each female bee prepares her nest and provides for her own family. There was not enough food available for that many bees in my park. Such large colonies are usually found on ranchland pasture farther west.

64

sweat bees on dandelions

My first step was to sit down and make a map of the park and of the neighborhood surrounding it. On this map I showed the large, dry patches of open ground and the location of the fields of dandelions that these little bees seem to prefer. It seemed likely that they would build their nests on open ground that was reasonably near several large patches of dandelions. And because they like to nest in ground that will dry quickly after a shower, it also seemed likely that they would nest on a slight slope or on the side of the rocky bank of a small ravine.

There were two spots on my map that seemed to be ideal for the little bees. One was at the edge of a baseball diamond, and the other one was on the bank of a gravel-covered drainage ditch that ran down the side of a gentle hill near a major highway. The baseball diamond seemed the least desirable spot of the two because of the activity there during the baseball season. So I made a trip to the hill and began my search.

At first there was not much to see along the banks of the ditch. The gravel and rough stone were excellent camouflage for any nests that may have been there. The only hope of finding them depended upon actually finding the bees returning with a load of nectar and pollen. Yet it was next to impossible to see a tiny bee flying over sand-colored stone and gravel. Now what?

There was just one last hope. I carefully stretched out on my back in the middle of the dry, rocky bed of the ditch about halfway down the hill. It wasn't exactly comfortable, but it was an ideal way to watch the top edges for flying bees. If any of them came to the ditch, they would be outlined against the clear sky for a moment as they flew over the edge.

In spite of the lumpy discomfort of the rocks, I soon began to enjoy lying in the ditch watching the many wild creatures scampering and buzzing around the rocks in search of food. A bright green lizard suddenly loomed up over the edge of a flat rock and stood surveying his hunting grounds as his ancestors had done from prehistoric times. His red tongue flicked in and out of his mouth as he slowly turned his head from side to side, searching for tasty insects. He disappeared then as suddenly as he had come. A moment later a sweat bee dipped down

66

collared lizard and sweat bee

over the edge of the ditch just above the lizard's rock—and disappeared into the gaping mouth of the hunting lizard! I had found my bees, but so had the lizard.

This unexpected turn of events called for a quick decision that it is always difficult for a naturalist to make. Should I interfere with this conflict between two of nature's most primitive living creatures? Or would I learn more by simply watching without interference? Since there would be nothing left of the bees if I left the lizard alone, I finally decided to evict him from his home. I scooped him up and carried him off to the bottom of the hill where he was released unharmed. He quickly vanished among the rocks.

Returning to the spot where the bee had been captured, I carefully examined the hard-packed earth between the rocks. The burrows were so tiny that it took half an hour or more to find them, but it was worth the search. I suddenly found myself staring into the angry eyes of a guard bee about three inches from my nose. Remembering the power behind those supposedly feeble stingers, I moved back a respectable distance and watched the small bees coming and going.

Other eyes were also watching the bees with great interest. Parasitic bee flies hovered over the entrances waiting for a chance to spray the returning bees with their eggs. A huge robber fly hung around for several minutes, then swooped down and carried away one of the bee flies. An ambush bug had slipped back into the shelter of the rocks at sight of the robber fly, but now he came back out into the sunlight to resume his wait. With so many enemies feeding on them, it seemed remarkable that the little bees were able to survive at all.

One bee, probably an old queen who had hibernated through the past winter, stood guard at the entrance to one of the nests. When a worker female would return with a load of nectar and pollen, the guard would step back into a shallow room at one side of the entrance and would let the worker into the burrow. It was still too early in the summer for the first males to appear, but the pollen that the little workers were bringing in would be used to feed the generation of males that would hatch from their unfertilized eggs. Only the old queen would be able to lay eggs from which the female workers would hatch.

Once the males had hatched and mated with the female workers, they would wander away from the nest to spend the remainder of their brief lives lazily feasting on the abundant nectar of the late summer blossoms. When the first cool days of autumn began to leave a chill over the rocky nesting ground, the fertilized females would either dig their lonely hibernation burrows near their old home, or they would simply build an extension onto the side of the home burrow. Here each one would build a separate apartment for the raising of her own young the following spring.

68

Though these little bees are often called solitary bees, you can see that they are in fact a very primitive type of social bee. When the young females emerge from the separate apartments or individual burrows, they will remain at the home nest and will join in collecting food and defending the burrow against their many enemies.

The desperate struggle for survival that these little bees faced continuously convinced me that there was more to gain from leaving them undisturbed than would be gained by digging up their colony out of curiosity. This time I left my digging tools at home whenever I went to watch them. With a large magnifying glass I was able to study the individuals coming and going from the nests. As for the life inside the hard ground, I was content to leave that secret for the bees.

Mother Hen of the Honey Cave

It was just before dawn one morning in late summer when a ghostly humming sound began drifting toward me from the edge of the swamp. It was so dark at that moment that the old logging road on which I stood was only a grayish-white strip that melted away into the humid blackness. Now I wasn't exactly what you would call nervous, but most of the hairs on the back of my neck were standing on end. I had come out to try to catch a glimpse of an occasional gray fox or perhaps a bobcat slinking back to its den at the first light of dawn. The humming I had not counted on. In spite of my desire to leave the area rather hurriedly, my curiosity forced me to wait on the road until the first signs of daylight slowly forced the gloomy darkness back among the cypress trees.

By the time I could see the other side of the road, there was nothing there for me to see. Nevertheless the sound continued as loud as ever. Whatever it was, it had to be not more than twenty feet away. The sound was coming from the middle of a gently sloping clearing at the other side of the road. With the comforting thought that at least the creature was too small to see, I cautiously pushed my way through some weeds and brush at the edge of the clearing and began a careful stalk. Within two minutes I had located the hiding place of the mysterious ghost in a field mouse burrow!

With a sigh, I sat down several feet away and watched the half-hidden entrance of the burrow. A few minutes later I leaped to my feet as a second, much fainter buzzing sound approached me from behind. It was only a solitary bumblebee. As I watched, she drifted unconcernedly down into the burrow. Nothing at all happened for several minutes, but finally two bumblebees flew out of the burrow and disappeared among the nearby trees.

As the first cool breezes of early morning began rippling the tips of the grassblades in the clearing, the ghostly sound gradually diminished and finally stopped altogether. Now I felt sure that I knew what my humming ghost had been.

Judging from the large number of worker bees flying back and forth from the burrow by now, there must have been some three hundred to four hundred of them living in that one field mouse burrow. With so many bees in a crowded room, the heat and humidity in the nest would build up to a very uncomfortable level during a night of inactivity. The workers would finally be forced to try to clear out the stale air. The only way they could do this would be to beat their wings for a fanning effect. The motion of so many wings would stir up the air enough to drive out some of the stale air and bring in fresh air to replace it. The most likely time for this to happen would be just before the dawn when the workers were awakening and were beginning to warm up their wings in preparation for the day's flights. With the burrow acting as a trumpet, you can imagine how loud the sound of three hundred pairs of bumblebee wings can be when they are all humming at the same time. There would be no such ghostly sound during the day because most of the bees would be out working. Their coming and going would keep the nest ventilated.

So many bees in a single colony would not be so unusual except that every worker in it had hatched that year from the egg laid by one weary queen. The lonely queen had probably hibernated beneath the bark of some rotting log during the past winter. When the first warm days of spring had taken the chill from the ground, she would have emerged from her hiding place to begin exploring for a suitable nesting spot.

A queen bumblebee must depend upon some other creature to dig her burrow because she is unable to do it for herself. I once saw a queen bee busily exploring all the possible nesting sites in a field at the edge of a pine forest. She flew in and out of a mole tunnel several times, coming out the last time with a huge wolf spider nipping at her heels. The next likely spot she explored was a mouse burrow that was still occupied. She never came back out of that one.

Once a bumblebee queen finds a nesting site that satisfies her, she begins bringing in loads of moss or dried grass with which to build her birdlike nest. Inside this nest she builds a little waxen cell and smears the inside with a mixture of honey and pollen. Once this is done, she partially fills the crude cell with more honey and pollen, then lays a single egg on top of this sticky food supply. Immediately after laying the egg, she seals this first cell and begins constructing a second one. The building material comes from little soft flakes of wax that ooze from between the segments of the queen's abdomen.

When several of the typically crude cells have been completed, the queen builds a wax honeypot and fills it with a watery mixture of honey and pollen. This will be her food supply as she sits patiently on top of her cells, waiting for the first of her young to hatch. The honeypot will also be used to feed the first little workers who will not be strong enough to leave the nest for a day or two. These first children are quite a problem for the young queen.

The first larvae to hatch will soon eat all their store of honey and pollen, then greedily demand more. The weary queen must then open the cells and feed her hungry young in much the same manner that a bird feeds its fledglings. Her first brood of four to eight bees will be all females. They will be smaller than those from later broods, probably because of the limited food supply in the early spring.

When the hardworking queen's first children do emerge from their cells, they are supposed to take over the routine duties around the hive while the queen lays her eggs. But the ungrateful little workers will often interrupt the queen's egg laying to try to steal and eat her newly laid eggs.

As the days pass, and more and more flowers become available to

bumble bee queen on underground nest

feed the hungry workers, they will at last leave their poor mother alone to tend to her egg laying. Each successive brood of workers that hatches now will be larger than those before them. By the middle of the summer a large number of the better-fed larvae will develop into the queens who will be responsible for building new colonies the following spring. Some of the smaller bees that hatch about this same time will be males that have come mostly from unfertilized eggs laid by some of the female workers.

Of course we could not expect life to proceed so uneventfully all during the spring and summer. Only a few of the many colonies begun in the spring will survive to fall. Some poorly selected sites will be flooded by spring rains or crushed by grazing cattle. Others will be destroyed by parasites or disease. Even those colonies that do survive will have a continuous struggle for life.

Of the many natural parasites of the bumblebees, perhaps one of the most troublesome is the cuckoo bee. This lazy creature cannot be bothered with building egg cells and stocking honeypots when it is so much easier to lay her eggs in some harder-working queen's cells. All the cuckoo bee has to do is manage to slip past the guards at the entrance of an established nest, and then she is usually accepted by the colony. Usually, but not always!

Some bumblebee colonies meet the threat of the cuckoo bee with direct action. As the cuckoo approaches the nest, the angry workers pour out the burrow and engulf her in a swirling ball of bees. As the angrily buzzing ball rolls about over the ground, the cuckoo sometimes manages to slip quietly out of it and run for the now unprotected nest entrance. If she makes it, she may be accepted by the colony because she will soon pick up the characteristic odor of the other workers.

Not all species of bumblebees treat the cuckoo with such open hostility. Some of them welcome her into the nest and then promptly try to kill her with kindness. They bring lavish gifts of honey and pollen which they smear over her body and wings until she is a walking gluepot. If she is lucky, she may be able to escape before she turns into a helpless, sticky glob. But most of the time she ends up as a glob.

73

You can see that individual colonies of bumblebees have different approaches to their problems. The same is true of individual workers from the same colony. Some are quite mild mannered, while others have a terrible temper. I have seen bumblebees visiting flowers which would not readily yield their nectar or pollen. Some of the bumblebees would become disgusted and go on to other blossoms. But one or two would lose their tempers and vigorously shake the stamens of the reluctant flowers, buzzing angrily all the while. Some take an even more drastic approach to the problem of deep and narrow flowers like the honeysuckle. They alight on the base of the flower and bite a hole into it, then suck the nectar out of the hole. The impatient ones are probably also the best fed.

Not all the bumblebee's problems are concerned with parasites and reluctant flowers. They also have a tremendous housing problem. The queen has enough troubles just trying to build a nest for two or three dozen young. When they number into the hundreds, the nursery becomes rather crowded. Finally the workers get tired of walking around on one another's backs, and they swarm out of the nest and gather in a little crowd around the entrance, as if discussing a remedy for the crowded living conditions. At last some of the more impatient ones begin to gather bits of dried grass which they pass on to those nearer the entrance. Soon the entire crowd is busily gathering and carrying bits of grass into the nest where other workers take it and begin lining deeper passageways to make more egg-laying chambers for their queen.

After months of hard work and repeated defenses of their nest against invaders, the time comes in late summer when the young queens and the small males must leave the colony for good. Soon they will mate and then wander away to explore the pleasures of the last flowers of the season. With the first hint of the coming winter the males will die one by one, and the sleepy, fertilized queens will dig deep into thick grass sod or hide beneath the bark of a rotted log. There they will spend the long winter in hibernation.

The dying colony will age rapidly in the autumn. The spirit of the remaining, elderly workers will begin to sag, and the poorly tended

74

nest will begin to fall apart. Small moths entering the nest without opposition will remain only long enough to lay their eggs. Their larvae will soon emerge to feed on the crumbling walls of the old honey cells. Beetles, earwigs, and velvet ants will soon come to complete the destruction. By this time the exhausted queen and her few faithful and ragged attendants will seem to care no longer. The brave colony that has given birth to the new life now sleeping in the forest will soon be nothing more than bits of dry bodies scattered among fragments of wax and overlooked pollen grains.

As I shook my head to clear it of these wandering thoughts, I felt a sudden chill. But overhead the bright summer sun shone down on the clearing as the unknowing bumblebees cheerfully went about their work.

Hunting Guide

Scientific Names: (1) *Halictus;* (2) *Bombus.*

Common Names: *Halictus* is the solitary bee, more commonly known as the sweat bee, or as the ground-nesting bee, and burrowing bee.

Bombus is the bumblebee.

Description: The **sweat bees** range from about one-eighth inch to one-fourth inch in length. Most are black with red, yellow, or metallic markings. They resemble the larger honeybees.

The **bumblebees** are about one inch long. Their thick bodies are usually rather hairy and are primarily dark brown in color with golden-orange stripes around the abdomen. They look rather like giant honeybees.

Habitat: Both the sweat bees and the bumblebees are widespread, though the sweat bees are found in the largest numbers in the far

sweat bee *(halictus)*

75

bumble bee *(bombus)* on red clover

western states, and the bumblebees are most abundant in the eastern central states. The sweat bees build their nests along the sides of sandy banks, next to gravel paths or roads, and in patches of dry, sandy soil.

The bumblebee queen may choose from a variety of nesting sites. Some prefer to nest at the surface of the ground, others choose the abandoned burrows of small mammals, and a few may even choose to build their nest in an old bird's nest or even in a strawstack. When they nest in the ground, they prefer firmly packed soil in a dry but protected spot. Few species will nest in rich organic soil or in densely shaded spots.

Stalking Methods: These are difficult insects to locate. First you should check dandelion patches on several days to try to find the little sweat bees. If they are not easily found at first, check the blossoms a few weeks later. Once you have found them regularly visiting neighborhood flowers, try to locate suitable nesting sites. Each such site should be carefully examined for the presence of flying bees. If you sit quietly for half an hour on a warm, sunny day, you will know whether or not there are any bees nesting in the area. They will be actively going and coming all day around a nesting site.

Bumblebees are located in the same way, except that they prefer red clover and tomatoes. Their nests are so rare that there is really not any very good way to go about looking for them. The workers from a single nest may cover several square miles of territory.

7
Armored Flesh-Eaters

Hunters by Moonlight

Some of the largest and most ferocious killers in the insect jungles would make excellent prey for a big game hunter except for their preference for hunting by night. In this respect they greatly resemble the leopards of Indonesia who sleep during the day and hunt by moonlight. Thus it is only on the rarest of occasions that the hunter in Indonesia or the big game insect hunter in America may witness the stalk and attack of either one of these terrible killers. At least the Indonesian hunter can bring the leopard to him by setting out live bait in a jungle clearing. But the hunt for the insect counterpart of the leopard is far more difficult. There is no trail to follow, no half-eaten kill to which the stealthy killer will return. There is only the darkness with its thousand flickering shadows and its silent struggles between life and death.

Is there no hope then for the determined hunter? Fortunately there is a weakness common to many of these night hunters. Even the king of them all, the dreaded green and red searcher beetle, is drawn irresistibly at night to the beckoning glow of an old streetlamp. Only the hypnotic pull of the light can interrupt its frenzied search for the living flesh which it must have to satisfy its gnawing hunger.

On a still, humid night in the early summer I accidentally managed to witness one of the several kills that one of these fierce beetles would make that night. I was collecting wolf spiders by the glow of an old streetlamp when several black wood-boring beetles began flinging themselves against the glass of the light almost directly above me. This was not an uncommon occurrence around a streetlamp at night, and so I paid little attention to the dazed beetles falling into the grass at the curb. An occasional nearsighted spider would make a lunge at one of them, perhaps mistaking it for a young cricket.

field cricket, searcher beetle, and wolf spider

An hour soon passed, and I was gathering up my collecting jars when a sparkling green beetle with red-bordered wing covers awkwardly dropped down through the air. It was a dreaded searcher beetle, the first I had seen that year. Almost as quickly as he touched the ground, he went scampering away through the grass as though he knew exactly where he was going. He almost ran over a large gray spider who angrily leaped straight at his head. Instead of ignoring the ill-tempered attack, the giant beetle whirled about and launched an attack of his own.

The startled spider was quick enough to get out of the beetle's way. Not even the bony fangs of the wolf spider can penetrate the shining armor of the searcher. The spider barely managed to escape with his life, though he scuttled away at top speed.

As quickly as the searcher lost sight of the spider, he spotted a young cricket that had its back turned to him. With no warning at all he rushed forward and pounced upon the unfortunate little creature. Within moments the hooked jaws of the searcher had crushed through the light armor of the cricket. The searcher was eating his little victim almost before I realized that the one-sided battle was ended.

The discovery of the lone searcher that night had quickened my interest in the other creatures that I had once considered commonplace. Except for an occasional automobile driving slowly down the poorly lighted street, there was nothing at all to indicate that the miniature field of battle which stretched out in front of me was actually situated in the middle of a modern city. It could just as well have been taking place under the cold eye of a full moon while dinosaurs stalked the trembling earth and the sparks of volcanoes filled the night with the smell of burning sulfur.

Standing in the shadows of the insect jungle that night, I could feel for perhaps the first time some of the anxiety and uncertainty that must be constantly a part of the lives of these jungle creatures.

Ghostly Keepers of the Flame That Never Burns

One of the greatest curiosities of the insect jungles is the surprisingly ferocious little firefly who discovered fire long before man did. In fact this fire is so remarkable that even modern man is unable to produce anything exactly like it. The flame burns with scarcely any heat and gives off a light that is fifteen times more efficient than the best light bulb in existence. But did this remarkable "invention" do the little beasts any good? They still eat raw meat even though man's less-efficient fire is now used for everything from modern warfare to baking angel food cake. As a matter of fact, these creatures seem to use their wonderful fire only for a signal light. It isn't good for anything else.

One evening I had gone out into my backyard with a flashlight just a little after dusk. The ground was cool and damp, so I sat in a chair to watch the flickering lights of the hunting fireflies who were making their takeoffs from tall blades of grass all over the yard. They seemed to be constantly rising into the air; yet they didn't move more than ten feet above the ground except on rare occasions. How could they keep flying upward all evening and still not get anywhere?

When my curiosity got the best of me, I began following closely behind one firefly. It soon became evident that he was using a peculiar trick that made him appear to be rising while he was actually only moving across the yard. He would rise up a foot or two, flashing his light briefly on the way up, then he would dip down to about his former level. In a couple of seconds he would again rise, flashing as he moved upwards.

Most of the twinkling lights seemed to be several feet above the ground, though I noticed after awhile that a few of them seemed to be coming from fireflies who did not want to leave the grassblades. I soon noticed that the flying fireflies seemed to be attracted to these stay-at-homes.

When it appeared that the flying fireflies were being attracted by the flashes coming from the grass, I wondered if it would be possible to attract them in the same way to my blinking flashlight. Everytime a flying firefly would flash his light near me, I would blink my flashlight in reply. At first nothing happened; then all of a sudden it seemed that every firefly in the air was coming toward me. It was rather obvious now that the fireflies on the ground were using their little signal lights to attract other fireflies.

Almost as soon as I turned off my flashlight, I noticed two little lights flashing from the grass just to one side of me. Some of the fireflies that had been attracted to my flashlight now swerved to one side to investigate the lights on the grass. One or two of them alighted in the grass, and the rest gradually wandered off.

Moving carefully and quietly so as not to disturb the fireflies in the grass, I got as close to them as possible. There were only two pairs of them there. One pair, which consisted of a male of one species and a female of a different species, was rolling and struggling on the ground. Finally the little female pinned down the male and killed him. As I watched in amazement, she began hurriedly eating the lifeless body of her victim. The second pair seemed to be more friendly, probably because it was made up of a male and a female of the same species.

The aggressive female fireflies apparently wait on the grass, signaling to the carefree males in the air above them. If a member of the same species answers the call, they will mate, and the female will soon afterwards lay her eggs on the damp ground or drop them over the dew-sprinkled grass. But if a male of another species shows up by mistake, he is seized and eaten without any hesitation. One insect is just as tasty as another, even if it happens to be a close relative. These hungry little females welcome unexpected guests.

Are you wondering how I knew that the fireflies sitting on the grass were females and not males? A careful study of most insects will reveal differences in body size, coloration, and shape between the two sexes. But in this case I knew that the grounded fireflies were females because they were attracting the flying fireflies. And in the insect world it is almost an unbroken rule that the females of all species attract the males rather than the other way around. The attraction may be a signal light, an odor, or a distinctive coloration. It is a little unusual to find females using their mating signals to attract food, but this is only one of the endless surprises of the insect world.

You might expect some heat to be produced by the brightly flashing signal light that the fireflies use, but if it got very warm, they might feel somewhat uncomfortable and less inclined to use the light as a continuously blinking signal. Actually this ghostly flame never burns

fireflies

or even gets warm to the touch. It is the result of a chemical reaction that has puzzled scientists for many centuries. Now at last chemists and biologists are beginning to understand the mystery and have been able to reproduce the effect in their laboratories (using purified materials obtained from the bodies of the fireflies).

The flame is produced by the almost simultaneous combination of four different chemicals: oxygen from the atmosphere, a mysterious substance known as luciferin, an enzyme called luciferase, and a highly reactive substance known as adenosine triphosphate. (The names are longer than the firefly!) As the flying firefly rises, he draws in an extra supply of oxygen that is used to feed the flame. In a fraction of a second, the extra oxygen slams into the molecules of luciferin. At the same time the luciferase becomes tangled up with these colliding molecules, breaking apart the adenosine triphosphate in the confusion. The result of this broken tangle of molecules is a silent explosion of light. Immediately following the explosion, the luciferin-oxygen combination is carried away by the blood, the shattered adenosine triphosphate is replaced, and the luciferase sits back and waits for more oxygen. It is really remarkable that such a tremendous yet harmless explosion can be produced within such a fragile body.

Even the firefly eggs bear the distinct, luminous trademark. Almost too tiny to see, the glowing eggs will lie on the ground or in the damp pulp of a decaying log for as much as four or five weeks before they finally hatch into equally luminous larvae.

The first occupation of these glowing, minute larvae is to find food. Each one begins its search almost immediately and will not rest until it locates and poisons a tiny earthworm or snail upon which it will feast for many hours. Tiny, poisonous fangs are used to paralyze the victims which are then eaten alive. They are conveniently digested first by the action of the poison, then lapped up as a thick and apparently appetizing soup.

The larva grows rapidly on this diet, finally reaching the stage at which it will pupate. Now it hurriedly spins a silken cocoon about itself and settles down for about ten days. When it emerges as a full grown adult, one instinct tells it to find a mate to insure the continuation of the species. The other instinct drives it to search for living prey. Only the female combines both instincts into one practical action by attracting males for mating and for a late supper—her supper. The males who survive will exist on a diet of fresh earthworms and snails.

Keepers of the Dead

In the ancient times when your grandparents were children, almost every church employed a sexton to help take care of the church and the church cemetery. One of his more unpleasant duties was digging graves. In these modern times churches still have sextons, though they rarely have any grave-digging duties.

The animals of field and forest have their sextons also, but the serious little gravediggers work without either pay or ceremony. Unlike their human counterparts, they seem to enjoy their work. Day and night they remain dressed in their greasy little black tuxedos, ready for the first faint call to come to them in the dark of night. When the call does come, they are always ready.

I first met the little sextons one hot summer night when a thunderstorm was looming up out of the northwest. I had gone out into my backyard late that evening, intending to bury the body of a young squirrel that I had found back in one corner of the yard. As I approached the spot, ragged flashes of lightning in the black sky lighted my yard often enough for me to catch glimpses of beetles, crickets, and wolf spiders scurrying through the grass in search of shelter. Though the rain was still miles away, they could already sense the danger.

Just as I reached the body of the squirrel, a particularly bold flash of lightning tore the sky apart and lighted my yard with its dazzling blue-white light. At that instant the dead body of the squirrel began twitching and jerking! If this had not been in my own yard in the middle of a large city, I would certainly not have stood there to see what else was going to happen.

With the aid of a flashlight I made a cautious but thorough examination of the body and of the soil around it. I was not too surprised to find two huge, black and red beetles busily moving the body back and forth as they dug into the soft earth around and beneath it. They would burrow under the body and scoop out the soil, then rock the squirrel until it gently settled down into the excavation. As the body began to settle into the fresh grave, the sextons carefully kicked the piled-up soil onto the top of it. Thus they were burying it at the same time that they lowered it into the hole. The soil was so loose and moist in that spot that within an hour only a pulsing mound of loose soil could be seen. Even after the body was covered, the hard working beetles were still not satisfied. They continued to dig deeper and deeper, lowering and covering their treasure until at last they reached the desired level. Or at least I supposed they reached the desired level. Before they were finished, large drops of rain began splashing down through the dusty leaves of some elm tree branches overhead. I cut off the flashlight and ran for cover myself. Moments later the rain began in earnest.

The amazing task that these two large beetles had completed in the space of an hour or two would be the equivalent of two men burying a dead elephant with toy shovels—in two hours or less! Even if this were possible, there would be the extra problem of laying an egg on it when the rest of the job was finished.

If the rain did not drown my two beetles that night, the female of the pair would have scarcely paused to rest before laying her eggs either on it or in a little hollowed out chamber next to it. The heat of the decaying body would soon cause the eggs to hatch; so there would have been no real need for the parents to remain in this cozy little grave except for the fact that the newly born larvae are at first unable to feed on the body. They will instead eat partially digested carrion that has been regurgitated by the parents.

Within a few days after hatching, the fattened yellow larvae are ready to spin a cocoon and pupate while awaiting the transformation into an adult beetle. Each one digs further into the ground, then stops to spin a cocoon. Here they rest for several weeks until the time for emergence as adult beetles. When the time finally arrives, each one crawls to the surface and stretches his wings for a few minutes. As soon as its body and wings have hardened sufficiently in the warm

sexton beetles burying squirrel

evening air, the little beetle flies away to seek a fresh supply of food. In a few days the young adults will return to the soil to go into hibernation for the winter, emerging the following spring to search for a mate.

What becomes of the parents of these young beetles? They are old now, no longer useful to their world. After the young have left the comfortable grave, the parents slowly make their way out into the light again. But by now they are covered with decaying flesh, molds, and tiny mites. Some of their legs are broken off, and they are maddened by the destructive action of the parasites that cover them. Now they turn on one another and fight to the death. The survivor is no victor, though. For he will soon crawl away to die a miserable death beneath the cover of the falling leaves of autumn. Only the young will survive the winter, never giving a thought to the time when they too will be old and useless.

Hunting Guide

Scientific Names: (1) *Calosoma;* (2) *Photinus;* (3) *Necrophorus.*

Common Names: *Calosoma* is the ground beetle, also known as the searcher beetle and as the caterpillar hunter.

Photinus is the common firefly, also known as the lamplighter, lightning bug, and glowworm (larva only).

Necrophorus, the sexton beetle, is also known as the burying bettle and as the carrion beetle.

firefly

Description: The **ground beetle** is about 1¼ inches long. The leathery wing covers are a bright, metallic green with a pale red margin. The body is rather flat and broad.

The **firefly** is a beetle with a body about one-half to three-fourths inch long. Depending upon the species, the body is dark

87

firefly larva

nymph

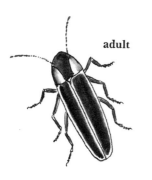

adult

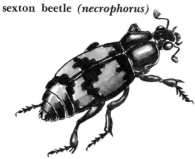

sexton beetle *(necrophorus)*

brown to pale gray on the upperside. The underside of the abdomen is a pale yellowish color. About half of the 120 species in the United States have a glowing tail segment.

The **sexton beetle** is about three-fourths to one inch long. It is a shining, oily black beetle with two broad, reddish-brown bands running across its wing covers. The thorax is smooth and bare above, but covered with a silklike, yellowish hair underneath.

Habitat: The ground beetle hides under stones and old logs during the day, coming out only at night to search for prey. As some of the adults hibernate through the winter, they may be found from early spring to late fall. The females lay their eggs in little mud cells in both the spring and fall. The larvae hatch out rather quickly, then almost immediately begin their search for mites and any other creatures smaller than themselves.

Adult fireflies hide inside flowers during the day or beneath the protective cover of thick, matted grass. The young may be found in and around rubbish piles and rotted wood in which they can more easily find the tiny insects upon which they feed. At night the adults may be found flying primarily over open grassland such as your own yard or a woodland meadow.

The sexton beetles hide under stones and logs during the day, coming out at night to feel the air for a delicate scent of their peculiar prey. Within a day or two of the death of a small bird or animal, any sexton beetles in your neighborhood will be attracted to the body from as much as half a mile away.

Stalking Methods: Ground beetles may sometimes be found hiding under stones or logs during the day. With the aid of a flashlight at night you may sometimes find them running up and down trees in which caterpillars have been feeding. They are probably the easiest to find under streetlights or near porch lights at night.

Fireflies may be found hiding in cupshaped flower blossoms. Occassionally they may be found crawling around on the petals of a rose or other flower during the day. At night they are most easily taken just after dusk or just before dawn. At times they will be attracted to a flashlight that is blinked at regular intervals of from two to six seconds.

Sexton beetles may be found hiding under stones and rotting logs or occasionally under piles of decaying leaves. At night they are readily attracted to the odor of decaying flesh of any kind. They will come to an old piece of raw meat as quickly as to the body of a dead animal. They should be handled as little as possible because of their fondness for decaying meat. There is always the possibility that they are carrying disease germs from their recent finds.

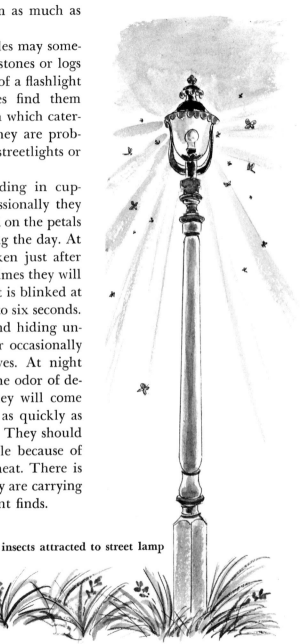

insects attracted to street lamp

8

Vampires of the Grassland

Terror of the Aphid Herds

You have seen how many of the creatures of the insect jungles fight their battles or defend themselves with their barbed legs, crushing jaws, poisonous daggers, or heavy armor. But what of the meek and apparently helpless little creatures who have no weapons or defensive armor? You would expect them to be as shy as the mule deer of the western mountain forests, hiding by day and coming out to eat only late in the evening and just before daybreak. You certainly wouldn't expect them to gather in large, unprotected herds right out in the open in the middle of the day.

The most helpless of all the creatures of these miniature jungles are the tiny green cattle who practically cover the leaves and buds of rose bushes every spring and summer. These little aphids, or plant lice as they are sometimes called, offer no resistance at all to their enemies. Yet they are almost impossible to destroy. I spray my own roses with insecticide every week, but by the end of the week there are just as many or perhaps more aphids on my plants than ever before. How do they do it? They couldn't travel to my garden from the neighbors' yards because only one or two out of several hundred can fly or even walk very fast. Their secret is simply that practically every female in the herd is almost constantly giving birth to living young, and practically every aphid is a female! They reproduce so rapidly that none of their enemies, including man, has ever been able to make much of a mark on them. One or two overlooked survivors is all it takes. Within a few days these one or two can produce many hundreds of offspring, and each of these hundreds can produce hundreds more. If they grew without any interruption, they would bury the earth in a single summer in a layer several feet thick.

90

Fortunately the aphids do get interrupted. Among their many natural enemies is a beautiful and quite harmless little insect with a delicately tinted green body, gauzy wings, and golden-bronze eyes. This pretty little creature, commonly known as a lacewing, would not dream of harming the aphids herself. She only wants to provide them with playmates to make their life interesting. Unfortunately for the aphids, little golden eyes has some unique ideas about playmates—her children are vampires. They do make things interesting for the aphids.

Late one evening in June I was busily spraying my aphid-covered roses when one of the golden eyes swooped down and began investigating the unsprayed bushes. I knew that she would not have the heart to pass up the juicy herds of aphids that were happily feeding on my expensive roses. Finally the little creature daintily alighted on the leaf of a Chrysler Imperial rose. As I watched from about eighteen inches away, she touched the tip of her abdomen to the leaf. It was barely possible to see the tiny drop of white fluid that she deposited before she lifted the tip of her abdomen up from the leaf to draw the drop out into a slender white stalk. The silken fluid hardened so quickly that it was already dry and rather stiff by the time she deposited an egg on the top of the flexible stalk. She repeated this performance several times, but it was so late in the evening that it soon became impossible to see what she was doing. It was too late by now to finish the spraying anyway, so I called it a day.

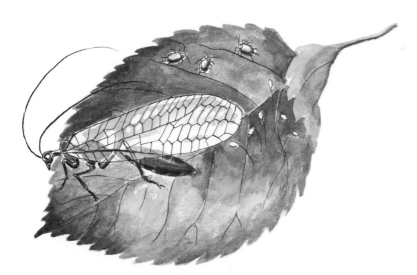

lacewings laying eggs among aphids (rose leaf)

The following morning I found more than a dozen of these little silk stalks on that one rose bush. Out of curiosity I left the aphids alone on this one and sprayed all the rest. Some of the few winged aphids would migrate to the sprayed plants, but it didn't make much difference. The aphid herds would grow back within a week anyway.

For two weeks or so I watched those little stalks as they gently waved back and forth in the breezes that crossed my yard. By the time I was ready to give up on them, I came out one day and found several inches on one branch cleared of aphids. The first of the larvae had hatched and was already at work bleeding his victims dry. This hairy, gray little vampire was shaped something like an alligator with a blunt tail. When I saw him, though, he appeared to be all mouth. He would snatch up an aphid in his hooked jaws, puncture it and suck out the honeyed blood, then throw the dry skin aside and grab another victim.

The other aphids seemed not to notice what was going on in their midst. They continued eating as though nothing were happening, until each one in turn was picked up and drained of its lifeblood. The little vampire, commonly called an aphis lion, seemed to be enjoying himself greatly. He never seemed to tire of drinking the aphid blood from dawn until dark. He would stop only long enough to shed his outer skin when his body became too large for it; then he would continue eating almost without interruption.

The strange feast went on for about two weeks. Then each of the several aphis lions on that bush gradually became more and more slug-gish. Finally they stopped eating and began preparing the private cocoons within which each one would be transformed into an adult. The surviving aphids just ignored all this.

It takes a little longer for the adult to emerge from the cocoon or pupal case than it did for the little aphis lion to grow to full size. But about sixteen days later the first of the pupal cases began cracking open, and a wet and bedraggled little lacewing crawled out of each one. In the late evening sunlight their wings and bodies slowly expanded and hardened until at last they were able to make their first hesitant, wob-bling flights. The ferocious little vampires had become creatures of great beauty, but only at the cost of hundreds of aphids.

The Fearless Robber Fly

Though the aphis lion will greedily eat any insect or insect eggs that it meets on a plant stem, it is limited by the fact that it is unable to fly or to pursue fast-moving prey. Most of the other vampires in these jungles have no such handicap. The fearless robber fly is one of the deadliest of these.

The robber fly is apparently convinced that there is no insect too large or too dangerous for it to capture and eat. These ferocious bearded pirates will attack and kill anything from a tiny spider to a full-grown bumblebee. In fact they will even attack and kill each other at the first opportunity.

I once saw a maddened hornet fighting with a female robber fly. The fly had not been able to get a good grip on the hornet and seemed to be having a difficult time killing it. In the meantime a male robber fly spotted the struggling pair rolling in the grass. He swooped down and stabbed the hornet in a direct and businesslike manner, paralyzing it almost instantly with a powerful poison injected with his beak. The ungrateful female released the dying hornet and killed her rescuer without any warning. It took her quite some time to finish both her prizes.

These highly efficient killers begin life in an egg carelessly buried in moist soil or even dropped in a crevice in a stem of grass. When the tiny larva hatches, his first thought of course is that it is time to eat. They are too small to kill very many other creatures, so at first they are forced to be vegetarians. As they grow larger and begin to range farther beneath piles of moldy leaves or through the crumbling tunnels of an old log, they will eagerly kill and eat any creature whose path they cross. Eventually these greedy little monsters lose interest in eating as the time for pupation approaches. Then each one crawls into a moist and protected spot within which it spins its cocoon.

The adult emerges some weeks later with a roaring appetite. Just as soon as its wings are reasonably dry and hardened, it will take off like a miniature fighter plane and swoop back and forth across the tips of the grassblades in its new hunting territory. The first spider, bee, housefly, or other insect it spots will soon be nothing more than a dry shell.

robber flies and hornet

Sometimes a hungry vampire will sit quietly in ambush, waiting for unsuspecting prey to come within range of its vision. The first creature smaller than a bird that passes nearby will be pounced upon and seized in its hairy legs while the vampire's daggerlike beak plunges through the victim's armored body. A paralyzing poison is injected to render the victim unconscious and to digest it at the same time.

The vampire has no crushing jaws or grinding teeth. He simply turns the victim's skin into a sort of spare stomach by squirting powerful digestive juices into it. While the victim is quietly dissolving inside its own skin, the powerful vampire carries it back to his favorite ambush perch and drains the skin of its spicy soup. The dried skin will soon afterwards be cast aside even as the robber fly is looking about for a fresh victim.

The robber flies must have been born without any feelings of fear of other creatures in their world, for they are so quick to attack even the largest and most dangerous prey that their courage seems almost foolhardy at times. Yet they temper this with at least a small amount of common sense. A naturalist once imprisoned a bumblebee and a robber fly in a glass jar so that he would be better able to see how the robber fly made its kill. But things didn't turn out quite right for the eager robber fly or for the eager naturalist either. The bumblebee, apparently a scarred veteran of many battles that summer, soon had the robber fly fighting in defense of its life. At last the exhausted fly collapsed and fell in a heap to the bottom of the jar. The bumblebee of course lost interest in her "dead" victim, and the naturalist lost interest in both of them.

Almost as soon as the naturalist opened the jar and dumped out the bee and the fly, the "dead" robber fly snapped to life and went blazing away across the grass. A few minutes later he was probably back at his old tricks of stalking his prey out in the open where he had more of a chance of being the victor himself.

On one or more of your safaris you will find a robber fly either scouting for fresh victims or lying in ambush on a shaded tree leaf. If you are patient, you may even be fortunate enough to witness the darting attack and the merciless destruction of its victim. Before you judge the

95

little killer for his cruel habits, you might remember that this is the only life he will ever know and the only life that his offspring will ever know. They kill only to survive.

Appetites with Armor

Have you ever picked up a little ladybug beetle and warned her to fly away home because her house is on fire and her children will burn? The warning in this old English jingle is quite unnecessary. Of the several species of young animals who are well able to take care of themselves, the young of the ladybug beetle probably lead the list. This little, harmless-looking, polka-dotted beetle and her brightly colored young are some of the most bloodthirsty creatures in all the insect jungles. They have been seen going through a herd of aphids or a patch of scale insects like a lawnmower through a field of clover. When they get through with their victims, the remains look rather like the chopped clover.

Like the lacewing, the ladybug beetle prefers to lay her eggs in the middle of herds of aphids or among patches of young scale insects. The children which soon hatch out are blue or black with orange markings. Their coloring resembles that of the adults, though they look and act more like brightly colored alligators.

Young ladybug beetle larvae begin feeding almost as soon as they are out of the eggshell. Sometimes they may not even wait that long. If there is nothing else handy, they will eat the cracked shell itself. They eat almost continuously for a month or more, stopping only long enough to molt when their skins become too tight for their growing bodies.

At the end of a month to five weeks of almost continuous feasting, the fat and happy larvae grow sleepy. They drowsily crawl under the nearest leaf and glue themselves to it with a glob of silk. Once a larva is firmly attached to the leaf, she spins a cocoon about herself to form a blunt, light-colored chrysalis from which an adult ladybug beetle will soon emerge. Soon each of the larvae will be sound asleep while their bodies soften in preparation for the remarkable transformation.

two-spotted and nine-spotted ladybird
beetles and larva with aphids

Though they are eager destroyers of many different kinds of insect pests such as aphids, red spiders, weevils, potato beetle eggs, and chinch bugs, these greedy little beetles and their half-starved young are rather uncooperative assistants for gardeners. Several times in the past year I spotted an adult ladybug searching hungrily for fresh meat. Each time I would gently and carefully pick her up with a grassblade and transfer her to the middle of my rose garden aphids. She would invariably turn her nose up at them and fly away over the top of the house.

Fortunately a few of the bashful ladybugs did stay long enough to lay a few eggs. It wasn't too much longer before the larvae from these eggs were crawling around looking for something edible. Whenever I found one of the creatures on an empty branch, I would carefully transfer the eating machine to the middle of an aphid herd. Then I waited for the action to begin. And I waited. And I waited some more. For some vague reason the larvae didn't seem to be the least bit interested in the abundance of food.

Farmers sometimes have similar problems with the ladybugs, but on a much larger scale. Because the ladybug beetles have the habit of migrating by the millions to isolated mountain meadows where they will hibernate for the winter, some adventurous people will climb to these distant meadows and harvest hundreds of pounds of these sleeping beetles. The captives are kept in hibernation by keeping them cool until it is time for them to be released in a citrus grove or in the middle of a large potato field or cotton field. Hopefully the beetles will eat a variety of insect pests when they warm up and begin to come out of hibernation.

One time an alfalfa farmer in California bought one million of the beetles and turned them loose in the middle of one of his largest alfalfa fields. Another farmer turned several hundred thousand of them loose in a huge field of peas in Wiconsin. In both cases these uncooperative little beetles woke up, stretched their wings, then promptly flew to neighboring farms to kill the insect pests there.

Except for professional collectors, the ladybugs have few enemies. They will unhesitatingly kill and eat many of the insects that are their own size or smaller. Their own heavy armor protects them from the

98

larger insects that might otherwise make a meal of ladybug steaks.

In the unlikely event that the ladybug is threatened by some enemy, she will fold up her legs and flop over as though she had suddenly dropped dead. When the danger is past, the little faker will go on with her own killing. The assassin bug is one of the few of the ladybug's enemies from which she cannot easily escape. This creature stabs the beetle in a tiny, unprotected gap in its armor, then sucks away the blood of its helpless victim, like a vampire. Even the most ferocious killers of the insect jungles seldom die of old age.

Hunting Guide

Scientific Names: (1) *Chrysopa;* (2) *Proctacanthus;* (3) *Coccinella.*

Common Names: *Chrysopa* is a genus of the lacewing, also known as golden eyes, stink fly, and aphis lion (larva only).

Proctacanthus is a robber fly, also known as the bee killer.

Coccinella is the common ladybug or ladybird beetle, also known as the ladycow, ladyfly, and ladycock.

Description: The **lacewing** is about half an inch long. Its slender, pale green body bears two pairs of gauzy, transparent wings that come together over its back when it is at rest. Its most characteristic feature is the pair of golden-bronze eyes that shine like flakes of gold when the creature is near a light. The alligator-like larva is grayish-brown with a rather long and broad abdomen that tapers to a stubby point. Its large, curved jaws are rather conspicuous, especially to an aphid.

A **robber fly** ranges from about one inch to two inches in length, depending upon

lacewing's larva

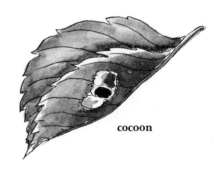

cocoon

99

the species. The body color varies with the species, but they all have the characteristic huge eyes of the fly family. The robber flies also grow a Mediterranean pirate's beard which is a thick collar of long and stiff hairs used to hold down the victims that might otherwise squirm out of the robber's grip. Most of the adults have long, hairy legs and a slender, gray body.

The adult **ladybug beetle** is about one-fourth inch long and looks rather like a small piece of enameled jewelry. Her armored wing covers are usually red or orange with two or more black polka dots on them. The shiny wing covers hide almost everything except her little black head. The blue, black, and orange young resemble the aphis lion except for their brighter colors. They look like a cross between a stubby alligator and an adult ladybug.

Habitat: From late summer until the middle of the following summer the lacewings prefer to live indoors. They will seek out a protected spot such as a basement or attic and will hibernate there for months. Apparently they are waiting for the following summer when the aphid season is well underway again. Only the golden eyes remain as a characteristic feature during the hibernation. The delicate green color of the body fades to a yellow or reddish color that probably serves as a sort of camouflage. In late summer they acquire their green color again and come out late each evening to lay their eggs. During the daytime they hide in grassland jungles.

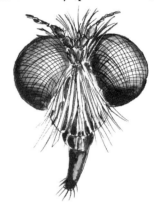

head of robber fly *(proctacanthus)*

twice-stabbed laydbird beetle

fifteen-spotted ladybird beetle

100

The robber flies often prefer to hide in ambush, using a twig or low bush as an observation perch. Occasionally they will make exploratory flights over open grassland, but usually they prefer to hide and hunt near flower beds or over low, wet ground where other insects are most likely to be found in large numbers.

The ladybug beetles hibernate under haystacks or strawstacks in the eastern and middle western parts of the United States. In the far west and northwest they hibernate in high country until late spring or early summer. During the summer and early autumn they may be readily found around vegetable gardens and flower gardens, and around fruit trees infested with scale insects.

Stalking Methods: The lacewing adults are most easily taken at outdoor lights at night. Where they are abundant they may be seen clinging to window screens of lighted rooms. The larvae are easily found on aphid-infested plants.

The robber fly may be found on bushes or low tree limbs in most areas that are attractive to other varieties of insects. They can probably be taken most readily by sweeping tall grass and brushy plants with a sweep net.

The ladybug beetles should be easy to find in young vegetable gardens and around plants infested with aphids. The young of the ladybug beetle are so brightly colored that they are quite easy to find in spite of their small size. They will be most easily located on aphid-infested plants.

shepherd's purse

101

9

Ruthless Bandit Kings
and Hungry Tigers

The Cicada Killer

The African hunter who turns around and looks up into the bloodshot eyes of the rogue elephant sneaking up behind him must feel about the same way that I did the day I unexpectedly met my first king hornet. I had been trimming some elm tree limbs in my front yard when a weak branch collapsed beneath my feet and left me hanging by my hands about twenty-five feet above the ground. The sudden movement of the tree limbs disturbed a two-inch-long wasp who swooped down right in front of my nose. Fortunately this peace-loving monster with a sting about the size of a hat pin was content to do nothing more than hover there and give me a long, cross-eyed stare. Then she darted away as quickly as she had come.

This had happened late in the summer, at a time when the neighborhood trees were filled with screeching annual cicadas who are the sole prey of this huge wasp commonly called the king hornet or cicada killer. As I climbed up onto the branch from which I had been dangling, there was a flurry of excitement in the leaves off to one side. This was followed almost immediately by the terrified screech of a cicada that the wasp had attacked. Seconds later the two fighting insects tumbled to the ground in a silent struggle.

Less than a minute later I could see the wasp straddle the paralyzed cicada. As soon as she had a good grip on it, she slowly rose into the air with it clutched to her body. Once she was airborne, the flight must have been much easier because it didn't take her long to drift out of sight. By the time I could slide halfway down the tree, she had disappeared down the street.

In the meantime the fat, greenish-gray cicadas resumed their raucous singing in the elm tree. As long as the wasp didn't bother them, they would enjoy the last few days of their lives singing and hunting for mates. But I suspected that the wasp would return to such a plentiful supply of game rather than waste her time searching other trees. Sure enough, within half an hour I could see her once again flying about through the branches like a combat helicopter. First she would rise several feet straight up the side of the tree trunk, then suddenly shift and buzz out along one of the branches. If the first branch didn't reveal a potential victim, she would rise further up the trunk and sweep out along another branch. It didn't take long for this determined hunter to find and subdue a second victim. Again there was the rush of wings, the angry buzzing and screeching; then the victor and victim tumbled to the ground.

This time I was on the ground myself, not more than ten feet away from the struggling pair. As I watched, the wasp stung her victim at least twice before attempting to lift it. As the cicada's body became numb with the paralyzing poison, the wasp straddled it the same as before. Beating her wings furiously, she slowly rose from the ground with her awkward burden and again rose into the air and drifted off down the street.

I had previously read that the cicada killer wasps are unable to lift their prey off the ground. Instead they were supposed to drag it up the side of a tree and then leap off into the air with it rather like the spider-hunting wasps. Obviously this wasp was unaware of the correct procedure for carrying her victim. She simply picked it up and flew off with it. Since then I have seen several of these wasps rising from the ground and flying over rooftops with their victims.

A killer as large as this one is not too difficult to follow even though she usually flies about ten to fifteen miles per hour. The one that I followed down my neighborhood street didn't have too far to go, either. She went to the end of the block and came in for a perfect landing near a jumble of limestone boulders in a vacant lot. The topsoil had been washed away from the slight rise of ground on which the boulders were lying, leaving a hard, reddish-gray clay exposed. I could see many large burrows scattered about among the shelter of the boulders.

cicada killer carrying annual cicada (elm)

My elm tree wasp dropped her cicada near her own burrow, then scrambled down into the dark tunnel. She ran back out a few seconds later as though expecting something to happen to her captive.

I was rather certain by now that she was planning to use the cicada as a food supply for her young. Remember the bee wolves and the ant-queen kidnappers? But would the cicada killer use the same kind of burrow and the same method for feeding her young? Rather than dig up any of these burrows I spent the afternoon sitting a dozen feet away from them.

While I waited there, I saw several more of these wasps coming back to their burrows with paralyzed cicadas. My particular wasp brought back two more cicadas, each of which was carefully hidden away in the same burrow. After awhile she seemed to lose interest in her burrow. Scratching some soil and debris into the entrance in what appeared to be a lazy attempt to disguise the burrow, she circled the area a time or two and left for the rest of the day.

There were probably four cicadas brought to this one female's burrow that day, three of which I had seen taken inside. I assume that the one taken while I was in the tree had also been carried inside. I felt I already knew something about the construction of the burrow. First of all it was probably a foot or more deep or the autumn rains and melting spring snows would have flooded the egg-laying chambers below. (Let us assume for a moment that she was laying eggs on her victims just as her ground-dwelling wasp relatives do.) It was quite likely that the cicadas were stored in separate chambers, each with one egg laid on it so that the ferocious meat-eating young wouldn't attack one another. This means that there must have been several side tunnels off of the main tunnel. Now, assuming that all this is reasonably accurate, we know what will probably become of the young ones.

The eggs were laid late in the summer which means that the larvae who hatched out would not grow to full size until about the middle of the autumn. If the full-grown larvae were to go ahead and pupate, they would emerge as adults at the beginning of the first hard frosts. This would hardly seem practical because there would not be any flowers for the young adults to feed upon. So it is most likely that the larvae hibernate within a cocoon, changing to pupae and finally into adults late in the following spring.

These were interesting assumptions, but were they correct? I could have found the answers in my favorite library, but there was a more exciting way to find them. With the amused permission of the owner of the vacant lot, I returned with a shovel and carefully dug into the abandoned burrow. By taking out a large section of the sticky clay, I could break the lumps apart and thus trace the direction in which the burrow had been dug.

About fifteen inches below the surface of the ground, and two feet away from the entrance, the sloping burrow opened into three roomy chambers. Two of these contained one cicada apiece. The third chamber contained two cicadas, one a little smaller than the other and probably a male. The other three appeared to be females. Though two of the cicadas had been damaged by the digging, the other two were in good condition. A careful examination of the underside of each one (they had been lying on their backs) revealed a tiny, glistening white egg.

To find out about the development of the young I could either come back late in the autumn and dig up more burrows, or take these cicadas home and put them in an artificial burrow in a cold corner of my basement. This artificial means of raising the young of burrowing insects seldom works out, but it was worth a try.

With the cicadas carefully held in one hand, I carried them back home and built two cup-shaped nests in a box of clay taken from the lot. Each nest was topped with an old coffee cup, leaving a crack at one edge for air circulation. A thick cloth was laid over the clay, and the whole thing was then covered with a sheet of plywood.

By carefully removing the cloth and then raising up one side of the cups, I was able to make daily inspections of the nests.

Three days later one of the two eggs hatched, and a tiny white larva could be seen feeding on the underside of the unlucky cicada. Surprisingly enough the entire cicada was consumed in less than two weeks. As soon as its meal had been finished, the larva did not waste any time before spinning its cocoon.

When the cocoon was completed, I cautiously removed the plywood cover and replaced it with a fine mesh wire screen. I had also removed the cloth from the inside of the box and now laid it over the screen. Just in case the adult did emerge in the middle of the winter, I wanted to leave it enough room to get out of the little chamber. On the other hand I didn't want it lying in ambush for me, either.

As the days grew colder and the clay began feeling icy to my touch, the silken case around the larva never moved. After some weeks the first snows came and I forgot about the box in the basement. When I remembered it early the next spring, I felt sure that the cocoon would be limp and moldy. To my great surprise I could detect faint movements within the silken case. By the end of March the movements had ceased and the case had hardened.

One day late in the spring I went to check the pupal case again after having ignored it for several weeks. There was a cicada killer clinging to the underside of the screen when I got there. It was apparently weakened from hunger and was unable to fly when I tried to release it outdoors. I tried to feed it with tiny drops of honey on the end of a toothpick, but the forlorn little monster showed no interest in the honey. The next day it was dead.

This was only one of countless cicada killers that could be found in my neighborhood that year, and most of these would die a lonely death. But for some reason the one that I had raised seemed just a little more important than the rest. I have never disturbed them since.

Tigers That Live in Paper Houses

The tigers that live in paper houses are not too easy to find in a city park unless there is a large, undeveloped area that is seldom disturbed. Perhaps that is just as well because these miniature tigers—more commonly known as yellow jackets or field hornets—are unpredictable and can be very dangerous both to man and to other animals. Even timber wolves will flee from them in terror, and there is not much that a timber wolf fears other than man.

As I have said before, you will sometimes find your prey in the most unlikely places. And there are times when they will find you, like the time the two thousand yellow jackets attacked me when I stepped into the middle of their nest. The only thing that saved my life that day was the fact that I was wearing tight bluejeans. When my foot went through the soft ground and into the middle of their underground nest, they came up over my shoe and started up my leg in a solid mass. The first wave had reached my knee before one or two of them managed to penetrate the tough cloth of my jeans with their stings. My first thought was that a rattlesnake had bitten me. My second thought was that perhaps I'd rather have had a snake bite me.

This was no time for an insect collection, and no place for an insect collector. Most of the hornets stayed near the nest when I went over a seven-foot wall next to it. The only ones that followed me very far were the three or four who had managed to get inside my shirt and were running up and down my back.

Before the numerous stings I received could stiffen my muscles too badly, I went back to rescue my collection of grasshoppers. Unfortunately the jar full of grasshoppers was surrounded by a cloud of yellow jackets, which presented something of a problem. I finally gave it up for a bad day and staggered home.

Two days later, when I was able to get out of bed by myself, I came back to make a hornet collection. Or perhaps I should say it was two nights later. No collector in his right mind is going to make a single-handed attack on two thousand tigers unless he can catch them while they are asleep. I chloroformed the nest that night, then came back the next day to dig up the broken remains of the paper house.

The hornets had not been destroyed out of a desire for revenge because after all they had a right to lose their tempers when I stuck my foot through their roof. But like the man-eating tiger that has first been crippled by a native spear, these killers were far too dangerous to be left alive in a populated area. It was not their fault any more than it is the fault of the crippled tiger, but they had to suffer the same fate. If a small child had fallen into the nest, the hornets might easily have killed him.

When I went back to the nest the morning after chloroforming it, I carried a shovel with which to unearth the broken paper house. Once

I had removed the earth from around it, I could see that the nest had not been too badly damaged after all. The outside was almost completely covered with a heavy layer of coarse, grayish paper with a large opening in the bottom. The shape was roughly round, though it had been distorted by the irregular outlines of the burrow in which it had been built. The inside of the nest was much more impressive than the outside. After carefully cutting through it with a sharp knife, I could see the separate apartments or layers that had been built one below the other, rather like a series of red wasp's nests stacked one on top another. The heavy shell had been built just around the outside of the separate layers, leaving just enough room for the hornets to move freely around the edges.

The cells in each layer were also very similar to those of the red wasp's nest. Because many of the cells are used three or four times, some hornet's nests about the size of a football have been known to produce as many as fifty thousand hornets during one single season.

Unlike some red wasp queens, the hornet queens do not work together in building a new nest in the spring. In the late summer or early fall they leave the home in which they were born and go out into the world to meet whatever fate awaits them. Sometime before the first frost they will mate, then seek the shelter of an old log or of a patch of loose bark on an old tree. Here they will hibernate during the winter, coming out the following spring to build a nest.

When the solitary queen finds a suitable nesting spot, either in a burrow or another hole in the ground, or perhaps in the sheltering branches of an evergreen shrub, she begins her nest with a spot of wood pulp. The hornet queen uses her powerful jaws to chew up bits of wood with which to make this crude paper. A short stem is extended from this first bit of sticky pulp, then the stem is gradually expanded to form a group of shallow cells in which the queen will lay her first eggs.

When the young hornets begin to hatch, the busy queen must hurry back and forth with sweet aphids, juicy caterpillars, and crispy houseflies. Her prey is not stung to death, but is crushed and chewed with the same jaws that are capable of tearing chunks of wood out of the side of an old tree or fence post. With the little spare time that she has,

109

cross section of yellow jacket nest

the queen busily extends the shallow cells to make them large enough for the rapidly growing larvae.

About six weeks after the first eggs were laid, the moist and still delicate young adults begin emerging from the cells. With what must be a sigh of relief, the tired queen now turns her attention to egg laying and leaves the flying to her new children. As soon as they are able to travel, they will begin bringing in fresh meat and well-chewed bits of wood and wastepaper. From that time on the queen will not leave the nest.

By the end of the summer the nest will usually have seven layers from which will have emerged several thousand workers and two or three hundred young queens and males. As the autumn leaves begin to change color, the queens and males will leave the nest for good. Soon afterward the remaining workers seem to realize that their end is near. They go berserk then, killing the young ones and tearing apart the nest.

In their last few weeks of life the frustrated workers will spend their leisure in drunken orgies around spoiled fruit, garbage pits, and carrion. Only the old queen and her few loyal followers will remain in the nest, and soon they too will be gone.

Hunting Guide

Scientific Names: (1) *Sphecius;* (2) *Vespa.*

Common Names: *Sphecius* is the cicada killer, better known as the king hornet though it is actually a wasp and not a hornet at all.

    Vespa is the yellow jacket, sometimes called a field hornet.

Description: The **cicada killer** or king hornet is one of the largest wasps in the United States. The length of the body ranges from $1\frac{1}{2}$ to 2 inches. The wings have a faintly metallic gold sheen, though they are transparent. The abdomen is black with gold markings.

    The **yellow jacket** is probably most easily

cicada killer *(sphecius)*

111

recognized by her aggressiveness and short temper. The half-inch-long workers are yellow with black bands around the abdomen and black markings on the thorax. The queen, who is sometimes three-fourths inch long, has sometimes been called the German hornet.

Habitat: The cicada killer will be most easily found late in the summer when the annual cicadas are emerging from underground and are climbing to the tops of the trees in your neighborhood. If there are any cicadas near your home, you cannot help finding them. They screech and sing almost continuously all through the day and into the evening. The nest of the cicada killer is a burrow that she digs in a dry location, preferably in clayey soils. The first burrows are prepared in the latter part of July. Though these are solitary wasps, many burrows may sometimes be found in one location. This is usually the case only because the soil conditions are better in that spot than in any other. The adults may be found in late spring and early summer, usually around fruit trees or other trees which have a sweet sap or flowers laden with nectar.

Yellow jacket queens hibernate during the winter under the bark of old logs and in woodpiles. They may sometimes be found in such locations in the middle of the winter, apparently frozen stiff. In the spring they thaw out and appear to be none the worse for the experience. The nests are almost always built underground, usually in

yellow jacket worker

yellow jacket *(vespa),* **queen**

112

an overgrown, brushy area, one where unexpected visitors will not be dropping in.

Stalking Methods: The king hornet may be attracted to honey or maple syrup brushed on tree trunks in the spring and early summer. If the bait is allowed to ferment, it will be even more attractive to king hornets —and to about five thousand other kinds of insects. In the late summer you can probably locate their burrows most easily by following one that has captured a cicada. If you are unable to follow it for the entire distance, mark the direction in which it is flying and then determine if there is a suitable nesting location anywhere within several hundred yards of the point of capture, lying in the direction taken by the wasp.

There is not any good way to locate a yellow jacket nest. Their small size, short tempers, and very poisonous stings make them very difficult to follow. The nests will very often be built in overgrown or inaccessible areas from which a rapid exit will be difficult. If a nest is discovered on one of your safaris, it should not be disturbed or approached too closely during daylight. Unless it presents a serious threat to other human beings living nearby, it should be left alone until after the first hard freeze in the fall. When the temperature is down near the freezing mark, any hornets that have survived the first frosts will be unable to fly. By this time the nest will probably be abandoned anyway.

campion

113

10
Man-Eating Kangaroos and Music-Playing Warriors

The Man-Eaters

In all the insect jungles there are few hunters bold enough to attack and attempt to eat live human beings. Of these few there is perhaps only one that has also been known to bring a thundering freight train to a screeching halt just because he and his friends were crossing the tracks when the train came along. If the frightened engineer was unable to stop the train, the insects would stop it for him. This monster and his close relatives have probably brought more death and destruction to human beings than any other insect known to mankind. Yet this destructive creature is a one-inch-long grasshopper commonly known as the migratory locust.

Once their march has begun, the legions of these earth-colored grasshoppers will stop at nothing in their search for food. In 1865 they even attacked an entire troop of United States Cavalry, seriously injuring one of the troopers with their ripping jaws. Before the trooper's comrades could come to his aid, his clothing was shredded, and his weather-toughened skin was torn and bleeding in a hundred places. When the grasshoppers were driven away from their living victim, they attacked the saddles, blankets, and even the oiled tents that had been set up.

As the hot summer wind drove them farther across the land, they swarmed across a solitary railroad track as a train approached from the east. The engineer recognized the danger and applied his brakes at once. But it was too late. With a shower of sparks the front wheels slid across the squirming mass of millions of grasshoppers, turning them into a slick grease that coated the rails and made the wheels useless. The train was still sitting there with its wheels spinning when the last of the surviving marchers had disappeared into the dusk.

114

In those days there was little that the farmers could do to protect their farms and livestock. The approach of the cloud of grasshoppers meant the ruin of everything the farmer owned. They would strip his fields in a matter of minutes, then move on to the pastures and crops of his neighbors. Of course things are different in modern times. Now the farmers are warned by predictions of the migrations in time to poison their fields and get their weapons ready. When the swarming cloud settles on the farmland, the flashing glow of flamethrowers and the sound of dynamite can be seen and heard for miles. But when the cloud finally moves on, no one can tell that its size has been decreased at all. The fields are buried with dead and dying 'hoppers; yet the countless millions of survivors will go on and on as though nothing had happened. In their wake the fields have been stripped bare.

Fortunately the swarms are becoming rarer now as more of the old egg-laying sites are being taken over for agriculture. The dry grasslands in which they breed are being occupied by vast herds of beef cattle whose crushing hooves probably destroy most of the eggs that are laid in the two egg-laying seasons of the year.

Even though it is unlikely that you will ever have the opportunity to witness a large migration of 'hoppers, you will find that the individuals are just as interesting as the marching herds. When I first learned of the serious damage that the grasshopper migrations can do, I took a closer look at the 'hoppers in my own neighborhood.

One day I was fortunate enough to surprise an egg-laying female while I was on a safari in search of some of the migratory grasshoppers. She was standing at the edge of a rocky path in a little patch of woods near my home. I had come up so quietly that she was not startled and in fact seemed determined to ignore me. Unfortunately for her, she was also ignoring the clumps of tall grasses on the other side of the trail. There, partially hidden by the grass, a pair of beady black eyes was also watching her with great interest. The eyes belonged to a little gray field mouse who was evidently out looking for his lunch.

The mouse must have seen me also because he hesitated for almost ten minutes. In the meantime the careless female 'hopper was busily probing the soil with the tip of her abdomen. When she finally found a soft spot among the bits of gravel, she quickly forced her abdomen down into the soil with a series of jabbing movements. While I could not see exactly what she was doing, I knew that she had three pairs of pointed prongs on the end of her abdomen. These were forced into the earth like a group of tiny shovels; then the abdomen would be expanded to push aside the soil. In a matter of minutes she had completed her little egg storage chamber and had begun laying her eggs inside it. As they were laid, the eggs were being coated with a thin, sticky glue which would soon dry to form a tough envelope. This would protect the fragile eggs until they hatched.

The little female was putting the final touches on her egg pod when the mouse became bold enough to make his move. He darted across the path like a gray streak and snatched up the grasshopper before she could twitch her muscles. A moment later only a puff of dust remained where she had been standing.

With my pocketknife I carefully cut out a small circle of earth from around the egg pod and lifted it up into my hand. I broke away the

vole stalking migratory grasshopper

crumbling soil and took my first good look at a grasshopper's egg pod. The glue was so sticky that many grains of sand and bits of humus remained stuck to it. Still, I could see the vague shapes of the eggs inside. There must have been about a dozen or more eggs in the pod, each being about the size and color of a grain of rice.

There was not really too much to see without tearing open the pod. I was sure that even then it would not be possible to tell very much. So I gently set the pod back down into the hole I had dug and carefully sprinkled some crumbling soil over it. Wind and rain would soon seal the pod beneath the surface of the earth, just as if the little curving tunnel had remained intact.

Female grasshoppers will lay as many as twenty-one pods with as many as twenty eggs each, so they don't really have the time to make a careful search for the best possible egg-laying sites. Of course it is a good thing that they don't because we wouldn't want all four hundred or so young ones to survive. As it turns out, only one or two of the four hundred will survive to adulthood.

The first obstacle that the young 'hoppers meet when they are hatched is how to get out of the cramped little room in which the eggs are laid. The body of the tiny insect is so soft that he cannot afford to get scratched by trying to climb out into the daylight and fresh air above. Fortunately for him he is covered with a clear but very tough envelope that makes him look like a little sausage with eyes. This covering will protect his

body from rough grains of sand as he forces his way up through the inch or so of soil overhead. The first one to emerge has the toughest job. The rest will simply squirm up through the hole that he has made for them.

The very next problem for the young 'hoppers will be predatory insects and birds against which the soft-bodied babies will be quite helpless. The protective envelope soon dries and is cast off. For several hours after this the ghostly white babies must remain exposed to sunlight and fresh air in order for their body armor to harden. While they are sunning themselves, they may be captured by carpenter ants, red wasps, or robber flies. As soon as they dry out and begin to change to a green or brownish color, they will hide in the grasslands and woody thickets until they are nearly grown. But here they are attacked by wolf spiders, snakes, and toads. The one or two that survive to the end of the summer are fortunate indeed. The grasshopper's life is certainly not filled with singing and dancing. He is too busy trying to stay alive until autumn.

When the first killing frosts of winter spread over the grasslands, all the grasshoppers will be killed. Yet the next spring there will be about as many as there were the year before because the female grasshoppers lay their eggs twice a year. A mild summer and autumn combined with an abundance of rain that encourages the growth of food plants will also encourage the production of a record number of eggs in the autumn. If there is an unusually large number of survivors from the hatching the following year, or if the following year does not produce enough tender grasses for the young 'hoppers, a migration is likely to begin.

During a particularly dry summer when the thirsty grasses fail to receive rain, the migratory grasshoppers begin to lose their bright green color. Over a short period of time they will gradually take on a reddish-brown coloration that matches the parched earth and the dried stalks of rustling grass. Now they will begin to gather by the thousands in open fields, moving restlessly across the land. Then one morning the air will be unusually warm, and there will be a gentle breeze rippling across the grassland. Soon the thousands will begin to take flight, and the thousands will merge with other thousands until the sky is darkened with their bodies and the fearful rustle of millions of wings will be heard for long distances.

118

At first the gathering clouds will take off into the wind, then turn and bank into rising currents of warm air that will carry them as much as two miles high over distances of up to fifty miles a day. When the air cools and the wind becomes weakened with its chattering burden, the cloud descends to the earth to strip it bare of every growing thing. When all else is gone, they will even attack trees, gnawing at the bark and shredding the tough leaves.

The destruction may proceed for weeks in spite of fires and poison baits. There are simply too many of them to be conquered by man. Finally the drowning rains will come, and the surviving clouds will break up into fragments that will soon be destroyed by eager birds and by the multitude of other natural enemies.

Over the years man has managed to destroy much of the good that Nature has provided, but only Nature has so far been able to control the menace that she has spawned. She does her job well. Soon there will be only an occasional injured grasshopper wandering to its death on the highway, or quietly lying down to die in the chill winds of winter.

The Musical Warriors

The art of training wild birds and animals to hunt and fight for man was originated in ancient times by members of primitive warrior clans who lived and hunted in the mysterious Far East. From these ancient skills have evolved the art of falconry, the sport of gazelle hunting with the aid of trained cheetahs, and the spirited and highly honored sport of cricket fighting. *Cricket fighting?*

If you are one of those bass fishermen who sometimes carries along a bucket of three or four dozen field crickets to use as bait, you may soon decide to use some other kind of bait. Those crickets could be worth from $50 to $100 each to a Japanese cricket fancier. One famous fighting cricket, appropriately named Genghis Khan, was made a Grand Marshal after winning $90,000 for his owner. When the cricket died, he was buried in a silver coffin with full military honors.

In the Orient there are professional cricket trainers who are hired to care for and train fighting crickets owned by wealthy businessmen. This

119

may sound silly at first, but how many fighters do you know who can earn $90,000 for their owners in one season? A good trainer knows all the proper exercises for his prize pupils, and he sees to it that they do their workouts daily. As a reward they receive such delightful food as rice and boiled chestnuts, fattened mosquitoes, and human blood. This certainly beats the American cricket's diet of grass, weaker crickets, and the linings of discarded shoes.

In the United States the crickets are better known for their singing than for their fighting ability. If you have ever had a cricket get into the wall of your house and keep you awake by chirping almost constantly, it might make you feel better to know that he wasn't any happier about it than you were. The noisy intruder was a male singing to attract a mate and it is not likely that he was having much luck inside the walls. The silent females prefer to live outdoors.

The adult crickets that you will find throughout the summer and early autumn spent their previous winter in the egg stage. As the days of early spring become warmer, the eggs begin to develop. In a few days a little lid on the top will pop open, and a flea-sized little cricket crawls out. He does not need the protective covering of the young grasshopper because the female cricket lays only a single egg in each burrow just below the surface of the ground.

You might think that crickets are lazy little creatures except when they are fighting, but the female cricket might take exception to this opinion. She may lay as many as five hundred to six hundred eggs over a period of several days, and each egg requires her to dig a separate burrow with the tip of her abdomen. It seems a pity that after all this work she will probably not live long enough to see a single one of her young.

All through the summer the growing crickets and those remaining from the previous year will live the joyful but sometimes hazardous life of wandering nomads in city parks and backyards. Perhaps it is their lack of serious interests during this time that has given them the reputation of carefree fiddlers. It is not until early in the autumn that they will make preparations for the coming winter. Even then they do not work at the job too hard or too long.

During the summer I have often turned over old boards, flat stones, and even dried leaves beneath which several crickets were hiding. As the long shadows of early evening raced across my backyard, these crickets would come out one at a time to slither almost unnoticed across the open grassland. Here and there one would settle down in a tuft of grass and would begin singing with reckless spirit.

It was just about dark one evening in September when I saw a wandering male cricket in my backyard make the mistake of coming too close to a singing male. Instantly the song ceased, and the former singer lunged at the intruder. The attack was so sudden that the intruder was struck broadside and whirled around halfway before he knew what was happening. He recovered almost instantly and snapped viciously at his attacker, but he was still off balance, and his strong jaws merely grazed the other's armored thorax. In a moment both crickets were rearing up on their hind legs like fighting horses, their bodies twisting frantically as each one attempted to bite off the forelegs or antennae of his opponent. A fraction of a second later they were rolling in the grass, biting and kicking like a pair of angry wildcats. This lasted only a very brief time before one of the two snapped off the lower half of his opponent's right hind leg. The fight ended at once with the injured cricket dragging himself away, leaving the winner to sing his shrill, chirping song of victory. It was impossible to tell which one had been doing the singing before the battle began.

While I watched the injured cricket, a wolf spider ran out from under a dried elm leaf and seized the helpless creature. There would have been no point in trying to help the little cricket escape. If the spider had not eaten him, one of his fellow crickets probably would have killed him anyway.

Most insects seem to be sluggish and unwilling to move in the chill winds of late autumn, but not so the crickets. One day late in that same year I saw a cricket hard at work in the dying clump of day lilies in my backyard. Using his strong jaws and forelegs, he was cutting out bits of earth from the soft ground. As the pile of soil began to grow around the shallow depression that he had started, he stepped over it and kicked it aside with his hind legs. Then he resumed his digging.

121

field crickets fighting

The digging went on for an hour or two before the cricket seemed satisfied. The burrow was hardly large enough to provide a shelter for him, and in fact his antennae protruded from the entrance. I felt certain that such a poor shelter would hardly protect a cricket for the winter.

When I returned to the burrow the next day, the cricket was again digging away as though he had never stopped. In a little while he stopped again and disappeared into the tunnel to spend the rest of the day there.

At intervals during the winter I would go out on a clear day to check my lazy cricket's burrow even though he seldom came out during the cold weather. On an unusually mild day he might sweep out his burrow, then sit out in the sunshine for a little while. Before long he would crawl back inside and go to sleep.

I must not have been the only creature watching that particular burrow, though. By the end of January I realized that my cricket had disappeared. The burrow was beginning to crumble, and bits of debris had settled over the unkept entrance. Somehow the yard seemed lonelier without him.

Hunting Guide

Scientific Names: (1) *Melanoplus;* (2) *Gryllus.*

Common Names: *Melanoplus* is the migratory grasshopper, sometimes called a locust, short-horned grasshopper.

Gryllus is the common field cricket or black cricket.

Description: The **migratory grasshopper** is one inch long. In the solitary phase it is green. In times of migration it becomes a reddish-brown color. There is an irregular black patch on the neck or collar.

The **field cricket** is about seven-eighths inch long. It has a solid black body with

grasshopper egg mass

123

grasshopper in flight

black or brown wings. It has the long, muscular hind legs characteristic of the grasshopper family to which it belongs.

Habitat: The migratory grasshoppers are most commonly found in open grasslands, especially in the Midwest. They may be found in fields or on idle lands where the soil is light or well drained.

Field crickets are common all over the United States. They may be found under brush piles, logs or under old boards and stones in almost any location that has grass and a little moisture.

Stalking Methods: Adult grasshoppers may be taken in the summer and fall with a sweep net that is rapidly swung back and forth through patches of weeds and high grasses. This method will result in the capture of numerous different species of grasshoppers. Individual species such as the migratory grasshopper can only be found and observed with a very patient stalk because most grasshoppers will take flight as soon as they see you approaching. Hunts should be made on warm, humid days for the best results.

Field crickets are most easily found during the daytime when they hide under almost anything that will keep them from being dried out by the sun. At night they are easily taken while they roam around in the grass beneath streetlamps or other outdoor lights. They may also be taken at their burrows if you stalk them very carefully at night, using a flashlight only at the last moment.

124

11

The Strange Tree Dwellers

The Wasps Who Grow Apples on Oak Trees

In the mountainous country of northern Arkansas the farmers each year harvest wild apples to feed to their livestock. There is nothing unusual about gathering wild apples for animal food, except that these apples grow on oak trees. Even this is not as remarkable as the fact that the apples are planted by tiny wasps early in the spring of the year. Some of the apples grow on the stems of the leaves, while others grow on the oak leaves themselves.

You have probably seen similar fruit growing on the leaf of an elm tree, on the stalk of a wheat plant, or even on a rose bush. They are not really the kind of apples that you would want to eat, though. Each one of them contains a tiny worm who is responsible for the apple's being there in the first place. You may have heard this strange fruit called galls, or they may sometimes be called rose galls, oak galls, or oak apples.

These galls are really not too harmful to the plants upon which they are growing, and in fact many of them are quite useful to man. In addition to providing food for the farmer's livestock, some oak galls contain so much tannic acid that they are used for making permanent inks or for dying wools and animal skins. Some galls produce so much honey-dew that ants and bees will gather in swarms around them to reap the rich harvest.

Galls may be caused by many different things such as tiny mites, parasitic fungi, and by little parasitic worms known as nematodes. But by far the most common gall is produced by tiny brown wasps. Their wings are so weak that they must experience a great deal of difficulty in flying from one tree to another; yet they manage to lay a large number of eggs in their brief lifetime. Finding a suitable place such as a tender oak leaf or a leaf stem to lay her eggs, the female wasp alights and plunges her stinglike ovipositor (egg-laying tool) into the plant tissue. The egg is deposited, and the little wasp wearily flies on to find another leaf.

It was once believed that the wasp stung the plant and that some poison from the sting would cause the plant tissues to swell to produce the gall. Now it is known that it is the larva itself that causes the gall by producing a substance that causes an excessive growth of the plant tissues in that small area. When the egg hatches, the tiny larva begins feeding on the juices of the plant. On this rich diet the tiny thing grows so rapidly that it would soon burst out into the air except that the plant has begun to grow rapidly in the area where the larva is feeding. The plant tissues swell up like wooden balloons to completely enclose the hungry little creature.

If the greedy little larva is luckier than most of her kind, she will become a wasp sometime early in June or July. By the middle of the summer only the gall will remain, with a tiny hole punched neatly through one side.

You might think that a wooden house with no doors and windows, hidden high up in the branches of an oak tree, would be safe from robbers. Unfortunately for the gall wasps, this is not the case at all. As soon as the galls begin to grow well, squirrels will eagerly creep out along the tree branches to gather them like fresh nuts. Woodpeckers will split the galls for the juicy larva within, and even field mice will tear apart any galls that may fall to the ground. Tiny parasitic flies also chew into the galls and rob nourishment from the larvae. Another wasp may penetrate the galls with its stinglike ovipositors to lay its parasitic eggs on top of the helpless larvae. If the gall wasp larva survives everything else, some farmer may come along and gather them to feed to his pigs.

If the spring of the year is cold and rainy, there may not be many galls produced. Stormy weather is hard on the gall wasps, though it seems to encourage gall making by some other parasites.

The galls produced by different species of parasites may take many different forms. Some resemble fresh fruit in both shape and color. Some are so fragile that they are as easily crushed as an eggshell, while

126

galls on red oak

others are so tough that they may break a knife blade if you try to cut them open. Regardless of the size, shape, and color of the galls produced by different causes, they all have one thing in common. Each parasite produces galls that are characteristic of its own species, and it is easier to identify the species that produced the gall than to identify the insect itself.

When you find out how difficult it is to find any of the adult wasps, you will realize why there is so little known about them.

The Flying Spear

The same mysterious jungles that produce the marching Amazon armies, man-eating kangaroos, flying wolves, and dinosaurs also produce the strange-looking ichneumon wasps, the flying spears whose young are so fierce that they will hatch out and eat their own mother if she does not lay her eggs quickly enough. Needless to say, the mother of these little monsters does not feel too loving toward them. If she is unable to find a suitable living prey within which she may lay her eggs, she will dump them overboard without a second thought.

I have found many of these skinny, long-winged ichneumon wasps in my garage each morning during the late summer, but it is only very rarely that I have ever been fortunate enough to witness one of them attacking its living victim.

As you know by now, it is sometimes easier to locate rare game or to witness unusual events when you are out on a safari for an entirely different purpose. This does not work out often enough to make it worthwhile as a hunting method, but you will get lucky at times when you least expect it. The first time that I ever watched the attack of an ichneumon wasp on its caterpillar prey was nothing more than a bit of good luck. I had just moved back into the shade of a thicket to rest from a morning of grasshopper collecting when I noticed two ichneumon wasps darting about through the sunlight-sprinkled foliage. At almost the same time I caught a glimpse of a small caterpillar crawling on a wild apple tree branch.

One of the two wasps saw the caterpillar at about the same moment

128

that I did, but the caterpillar had seen the wasp first. Recognizing its immediate danger, the fat little caterpillar reared up in alarm and began frantically weaving back and forth in what must have been intended to be a threatening gesture. Apparently it did bluff the wasp for a moment or two because she appeared to be hesitant about attacking a creature several times larger than herself. On the other hand she didn't really have too much choice because the little time-bomb eggs within her would soon be hatching out if she didn't make a gift of them to someone else.

It would have been too dangerous for the little wasp to simply drop out of the air onto the thrashing caterpillar, so she alighted on the leaf on which her intended prey had been eating. With her antennae quivering nervously and her wings trembling with excitement, she danced about on the leaf until the caterpillar appeared to be confused. After several minutes of this watching and waiting, the caterpillar began to weaken from its continuous efforts. As soon as its weaving slowed down, the wasp would made a halfhearted dash toward it, then retreat just as quickly.

Of course these pretended attacks made the poor caterpillar more nervous than ever, and he increased the rate of his weaving and thrashing until he finally became too weak to keep it up. Without a moment of further delay, the excited little wasp bounded into the air on blurred wings and dropped onto the back of the caterpillar. She plunged her long, spear-shaped ovipositor into the caterpillar's tough back, then rode him like a cowboy on a bucking brahma bull. It took only a few seconds for her to unload her frightful eggs into the weakened caterpillar; then she darted off into the air and disappeared into the thicket.

With what must have been a sigh of relief, the caterpillar settled down now and rested for a few minutes before getting up enough energy to resume its feeding. To the caterpillar the danger seemed to be past now. He could know nothing about the living death planted within his body.

The fearful little eggs are self-multiplying. If the caterpillar is large enough, the cells of the eggs break up into several individual groups

129

ichneumon wasp and fall cankerworm (apple)

so that many wasp larvae hatch from what had originally been a single egg. But if the caterpillar is small, the eggs hatch without this unusual cell separation.

Sometimes the caterpillar never seems to realize that he has guests in his living room. He will go ahead and spin his cocoon as though he

130

were living alone. But when the cocoon finally opens, only ichneumon wasps will emerge. The only thing left inside the hardened silk case will be one slightly used caterpillar skin.

There are many different sizes and shapes of flying spears or ichneumon wasps. One of the largest of these has an ovipositor that is capable of penetrating through two inches of solid wood. Sometimes this may be a disadvantage to the wasp when she finds that she cannot pull it out again. You can find these wasps in many areas where wood-boring beetles live and especially around old logs in the fall of the year.

I found the largest numbers of the long-tailed beetle larva hunters in a swampland. These ichneumon wasps may have a body an inch or more in length, trailed by three hairlike spears that may be as much as five inches long. One day I had the rare opportunity to watch a whole squadron of these reddish-brown wasps attacking an old log half-buried in the swamp mud. Much of the bark of the log had fallen off, exposing what must have been over a hundred holes made by wood-boring sawfly larvae. A find like this was more than one ichneumon wasp could handle, so it was not too surprising that about a dozen of them were hovering over the juicy find. Somewhere within that five or six hundred pounds of solid wood were more than enough larvae to take care of the needs of these female flying spears. They were not wasting any time taking advantage of it.

Using their antennae to sniff out the exact location of the unsuspecting larvae within their wooden tunnels, the wasps were settling down one by one to begin their drilling operations. They were so intent on their work that my approach to one end of the log scarcely caused a flutter of alarm among them. Most of them simply ignored me.

One of the wasps closest to me had spread out her middle and hind legs to brace herself, but had tucked her forelegs up under her chin in an attitude of great concentration. Her abdomen was lifted high into the air and curved over and downwards toward the wood. The three parts of the ovipositor were stretched as high as possible, then plunged down into the surface of the wood.

We are not certain just how the wasps penetrate the wood with their ovipositors, but apparently they have learned the secret well. With only

131

a few minutes of drilling, the pointed ovipositor is driven down into an occupied burrow and into the soft body of the sawfly larva. Occasionally the prey is injected with a paralyzing poison, though not always. In either case it will be hard on the wasp if her prey begins to move away. If her ovipositor ever gets bent out of shape, she will be stuck for good.

As a matter of fact, some members of this particular species do get stuck on occasion. When they do, there is no hope for them. Their only consolation is that they have probably already laid their eggs by the time they realize that they are stuck to the log. If the end of the ovipositor becomes wedged in the wood when it has been pulled back out of the burrow, the little wasp is really in trouble. The eggs left inside of her abdomen will soon be hatching and her children will make a meal of her.

Fortunately for the wasps that I was watching, not one ran into any real trouble. One of them was stuck for several minutes, but finally succeeded in withdrawing her ovipositor. Just to make sure that it didn't happen again, she carefully cleaned it off by drawing it through a V formed by her crossed hind legs. She repeated this until she seemed satisfied, briefly wiped off her sensitive antennae, then rose into the air and flew around the surface of the log in search of more prey. It would have been hard to say whether she was excited about making such a rich find, or whether she was just anxious to get rid of her eggs.

Carpenters Who Live in Trees

I don't really mind the carpenters who live in the trees in my backyard. The thing that does bother me is that some of them want to live in my house with me, and my house just isn't large enough to share with five hundred carpenters. They keep on insisting, though. One day I found a group of them living inside my garage window. The window had been stuck so tight that I had to get an axe to loosen it. That loosened it all right. It also loosened a large colony of the big, black carpenter ants who had finally managed to get into the house after all. They seemed rather irritated by my unannounced visit.

You might think that any self-respecting ant would prefer to live in

132

the ground, but carpenter ants are different. Their huge jaws are so powerful that they use them to crush wood fibers as they bore their way through tree trunks or into the beams and foundations of houses. Large rooms are cut from wood, and sawdust is then pushed back through the winding tunnels and out of the entrance. This makes a very secure home for the large ants until their tunneling weakens the structure so that it falls in, or until the insect exterminator comes out to gas the network of tunnels.

With their combination of powerful jaws and heavy armor, the carpenter ants have few natural enemies. And even these few are prevented from entering the tunnels because one of the workers uses his head to plug up the entrance while the rest are out foraging. When the food gatherers return to the colony, they had better remember the password because the stubborn guard plugging the entrance won't let them inside until they beat him over the head the correct number of times with their antennae. Any worker with a poor memory would probably be kept at home!

In the spring or early summer the colony will produce hundreds of inch-long queens who will soon leave their home forever. Once out in the warm sunlight they will mate with the smaller flying males from their own or other colonies, then drift away in search of a building site. Only a few of these will survive the hazards of the search, and of these some will become very frustrated before the search is over. The most puzzled queen carpenter ant that I ever saw was running up and down a metal door frame in a concrete-walled room full of iron pipe. I have often wondered what ever became of her.

Those queens who do find a nice wooden house, a dying tree, or an old rotted log will be the lucky ones. Now they can spend several weeks cheerfully working from dawn until dusk, chewing out wooden tunnels, laying eggs, and gathering food for themselves and for their larvae.

When the children are grown and go forth in search of food for their poor, ragged mother, the exhausted queen can settle back and contentedly spend the rest of her days in continuous egg laying. I sometimes wonder if they don't envy the guard who spends his days lazily plugging the tunnel entrance and watching the world go by.

black carpenter ants in nest with pupae, larvae, and eggs

Hunting Guide

Scientific Names: (1) *Amphibolips;* (2) *Ophion* and *Megarhyssa;* (3) *Camponotus.*

Common Names: *Amphibolips* is the gall wasp, sometimes known as the oak apple wasp. Entomologists (insect specialists) also call them cynipids because they belong to a family with the scientific name of Cynipidae.

Ophion is the caterpillar-hunting ichneumon wasp, and *Megarhyssa* is the sawfly larva hunter. The common names of both are the same. They are called ichenumon wasps or ichneumon flies, though they are neither true wasps nor flies. However, they are close relatives of the wasp family.

Camponotus is the carpenter ant, sometimes called the black carpenter ant.

Description: The **gall wasp** is from 1/64 to ⅛ inch long. The body color may be a shining black, dark maroon, bluish, yellowish, or brown depending upon the species. The rather spiny, fruitlike galls that they cause are a pale yellow to pale red color.

The caterpillar-hunting **ichneumon fly** is about 5/6 inches long. The body color is light brown. The long, slender abdomen is tipped with a short, stingerlike ovipositor. The sawfly larva-hunting ichneumon is about one inch long and has three thread-like ovipositors that may be as much as five inches long. This is a reddish-brown to orange-colored wasp with slight black and red markings. The wings bear brown spots.

The **carpenter ant** workers are from ¼ inch to ½ inch long. They are solid black

gall wasp *(amphibolips)*

ichneumon wasp *(megarhyssa)*

carpenter ant *(camponotus)*, **worker**

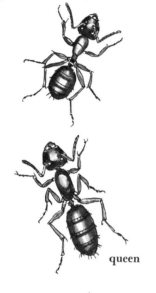

queen

winged male

with grayish-black rings around the abdomen. The winged queens range from 5/8 inch to nearly one inch in length. The wings are dropped after the mating season.

Habitat: The gall wasp is found chiefly around the oak trees on which the female lays her eggs. Because of their tiny size, it is unlikely that you will ever find one laying her eggs. Some species may be found around wild roses.

The ichneumon wasps are found around fallen trees and in thickets where caterpillars feed during the spring and summer.

Carpenter ants prefer rotted logs, but may also nest in dead trees, telephone poles, fence posts, and houses. They may often be seen running up and down the trunks of healthy trees.

Stalking Methods: Gall wasps are almost impossible to find in the adult stage because of their size. The easiest way to collect them is to remove gall-bearing leaves early in June before the wasp larvae have emerged as adults.

Ichneumon wasps will come to lights at night in the late spring and early summer. They may also be found by making periodic checks of old logs late in the summer.

Carpenter ants may be found rather easily in the eastern half of the United States. Foraging workers may be seen near rotted logs and on the trunks of trees. They can be followed to the nest by a patient stalker.

136

12

Hunters and Trappers
of the Vacant Lot Deserts

The Lion Who Walks Backwards

In the vast forests of African game preserves, native poachers sometimes dig huge pits along well-traveled animal trails. The bottom of each pit is studded with sharpened stakes, and the top is covered over with tree branches and coarse grasses. The trap is crude and primitive, but it works reasonably well. Sometimes it works so well that the poacher forgets where all of them are, then falls into one of them himself.

You will find similar traps in sandy fields and vacant lots in America, but these American traps are far better designed and much more effective in catching careless game. The major difference between the traps in America and those in Africa is that the American ones are dug by the lion who walks backwards. This little lion never falls into his own trap. He can't. He lives inside it.

The day that I followed the marching Amazon ant army I saw two of the Amazons topple over the edge of the conical sand pits dug by this hairy bodied ant lion. Though the half-inch-long ant warriors were almost twice as large as the trappers, they were quickly subdued and pulled beneath the surface of the sandy earth.

As much as I wanted to stay and watch the struggle between these two powerful jawed adversaries, I had waited too long to lose track of the Amazons. By the time the slave-taking raid was over, the sandpits were quiet again. The dried shell of one of the trapped Amazons lay at one side of the pit into which it had fallen, but inside the pit itself not a thing could be seen. Not a grain of sand was moving to indicate that a fat, hairy lion lay in ambush beneath the sand at the bottom of the pit.

Though it was getting dark by the time I had returned to the vicinity of the pits, I stayed long enough to dislodge a tiny shower of sand grains to imitate the struggles of a trapped victim. Instantly a pair of cruel, hooked jaws protruded from the sand. A moment later the head and part of the body of the ugly lion appeared. The thing turned from one side to the other, gnashing its jaws at the empty air. Then as suddenly as it had appeared, it withdrew into the sand, pausing only to flip its head a time or two to throw out the loose sand.

Of course I was back the next day, determined to stay long enough this time to see exactly what happened to the victims who dropped in for dinner. One thing that I have learned on my insect safaris is that there is no substitute for patience. I sat for two or three hours near the sandpits without seeing a single movement within them. An occasional insect did wander by on some important mission, but none of them came close to the pits.

Eventually a large, reddish-brown and black velvet ant came scurrying over the sandy ground in obvious search of fresh meat. This wingless female wasp is only half an inch long, but her sting is so powerful that she is greatly feared by other insects and by large mammals. It was understandable that this bold creature was quite careless in her hunting. That was her first mistake. She ran over the edge of a large pit that must have been three inches across. Down one side she went and halfway up the other side before the treacherous sand grains rolled out from under her feet and sent her sliding to the bottom of the pit and into the waiting jaws of the lion.

That was only the beginning. The ant lion's jaws snapped shut on the furry armor, but the velvet ant pulled herself loose almost without effort. Again she ran part way up the steep side of the pit and slid back down to the bottom. In the meantime the ant lion disappeared to think things over. He had probably never tackled any prey that could pull out of his jaws so easily. When the ant lion again stuck his head out of the sand and snapped at his elusive prey, the angry velvet ant leaped onto the bristly head of her attacker and swung her long and highly poisonous sting directly at the tormenting jaws. The ant lion ducked out of the way, then rapidly flicked his head up and down in the sand. This showered his adversary with sand until she became so

138

ant lion and velvet ant

confused she couldn't decide what to do. She was getting worried now.

When the velvet ant gave up on her attack and again ran up the side of the pit, she came within a quarter of an inch of escaping. The ant lion had lost his temper now and seemed determined to make a meal out of his tough enemy. Just as the velvet ant was almost within reach of the edge, a shower of sand grains was flicked up onto her back. She was so excited that the flying sand caused her to lose her grip and slide back into the jaws of death.

This time the ant lion was ready. He seized her abdomen in his needle-tipped jaws and instantly injected a paralyzing poison into her. The injection almost immediately began to take effect, and the velvet ant doubled up with pain and twisted her body with such force that the ant lion was dragged half out of his sandy cover. This was the last convulsive struggle of the velvet ant. Within seconds she was lying lifeless in her killer's jaws.

As though this were the most usual thing in the world for the little ant lion, he casually backed into the sand with his furry-bodied victim still held tightly in his jaws. An hour later the little killer reappeared with a shrunken, reddish-brown shell. With a quick toss of his head he threw the remains out of the pit and set about to repair the damage that had been done. A few minutes later the pit was exactly the same as it had been when I first arrived that morning.

Curious how the ant lion is able to construct such a perfectly conical pit simply by flicking sand grains up into the air, I took a tiny twig and tried to imitate the action by flicking sand away from one spot on the ground. All I got for my trouble was a crude, rounded hole in the ground. Obviously there was some trick involved even though it had seemed that the ant lion had been doing nothing more with his head than I had done with the twig. It would not have been much of a problem to find the answer in a reference book, but it would be more fun to learn it from the ant lion himself. Taking out my pocketknife, I slipped the blade down into the bottom of the pit and flicked the little ant lion out of the sand.

The little monster was unbelievably ugly. He was only about one-fourth inch long, but his body was covered with coarse bristles and what

140

looked like hundreds of little warts. The thick, flat head was decorated with huge, curved jaws that could kill just about any prey small enough to be trapped in the pit. As much as I disliked the velvet ants, I couldn't help pitying the one that had met its fate in the jaws of this horrible creature.

The ant lion didn't hold still for a careful examination, though. As soon as he found himself stranded on flat ground, he began shuffling backwards in a tight little circle. The flattened, spadelike end of his abdomen dipped into the loose sand and caused it to be forced up over his back and onto his head. As soon as he felt the weight of the sand on his head, he gave it a sudden flick that threw the sand grains several inches away. As the circling and head flicking continued, the ant lion was gradually sinking into the sand. The farther down he went, the more the sand would cave in from all sides onto his head. It would be just as quickly flicked over the edge of the deepening pit.

At the rate the ant lion was sinking back into the sand, it probably wouldn't have taken him more than half an hour to dig a new pit except that he ran into a pebble about halfway down. This was something that neither of us had expected. I was about to transfer the little monster to a better patch of sand because I knew that this pebble would interfere with the construction of his pit. He didn't seem to be too worried about it, though. By the time I had selected a better site for him, he had tunneled under the pebble and was lifting it up onto his back. The pebble was larger than he was, but he was so powerful that it didn't seem to bother him at all. The bristles on his back kept his burden from rolling off as he carefully backed up the partially completed side of his pit and tossed the pebble to one side. Then he slid back down to resume his digging. Soon the sand had slid down enough to erase the hole that had been left when the pebble was removed. By the time the ant lion was through, his pit was identical to those of his neighbors.

The ant lion is the larva of a flying insect known simply as the adult ant lion. From the description of the larva, you would imagine that the adult must be an equally horrible creature. But if you imagined that it would be some kind of monstrous killer, you would be completely

141

wrong. Actually, the adult ant lion seldom eats, and even then she probably captures only small insects such as gnats. Instead of being ugly, she rather looks like a delicate and slender-bodied damselfly.

The adult female ant lion flies about late in the evening, dropping her eggs in protected sandy locations where the hatching larvae will have the greatest chance for survival. The young are quite small at first, and so are the pits that they dig. But as they grow to full size over a period of two to three years, they gradually increase the size of the pits that they build. This probably helps to limit the size of the prey that they capture because large and dangerous prey can easily escape from the tiny pit of a very young larva. Only insects small enough for it to subdue will be trapped there.

Eventually the ant lion will spin a marble-shaped cocoon down under the sand. Several weeks later it will emerge into the warm summer sunlight as an adult with only a few weeks left to live. One of the great mysteries of nature is how the ant lion can build its cocoon underneath the sand without getting a single grain of sand inside it. The way it is done must be a remarkable feat, but it is not too surprising that such a wonderful little engineer is able to accomplish it all by himself. He may be a monster, but he is a smart little monster.

The Foreign Invaders

In 1891 the city of New Orleans, Louisiana, was invaded by a small army of soldiers who came in on freighters from Argentina and Brazil. From this port city the army spread throughout the South, bringing death and destruction in its wake. As the soldiers expanded their territories, they were met by other armies defending their own homes, but the invaders quickly overcame all opposition.

Perhaps the most remarkable thing of all is that these foreign armies are still fighting their battles in the southern half of the United States. If you live in this part of the country, there may even be an army of them camped out in your backyard. These are the armies of the militant Argentine ants, the only ants in the United States who fight in well-organized groups against which the much larger native ants are

142

helpless. Though these warriors may be as little as one-tenth inch long, they are seldom beaten in open combat.

Of the occasional large nests of the Argentines that I had found in northern Louisiana, most of them were minding their own business. There were few other creatures who wanted to take a chance on getting into an argument with them because you don't fight with one warrior. You might start out that way, but you would be quickly surrounded and charged by an army of his fellows.

One day I came across a particularly large nest of Argentine ants in the shadow of a half-rotted pine log. A long trail of warrior-workers led from the nest out over the hard, red clay soil of a logging road and on into the pine forest on the other side. The trail wound across the ground littered with pinestraw over a distance of thirty or forty yards to the body of a dead rabbit. The little carcass was practically covered with ants gathering the meat to take back to the nest. If they had not been interrupted, they might have stripped away most of the flesh before nightfall.

About fifty or sixty feet away was a nest of the hot-tempered fire ants, another South American import to the United States. While I was watching the collection of meat by the Argentines, two or three fire ant scouts were attracted to the rabbit. A shifting breeze had earlier been blowing from their nest to the body, so they had not scented it before now.

Getting as close to the rabbit as they dared, the scouts eagerly waved their antennae to pick up the inviting smell of fresh meat. With great caution they circled part of the way around the rabbit, then wheeled about and ran back to their huge mound nest. If the Argentines noticed this activity, they did not show any sign of it. I knew that it was only a matter of time now before I would be able to witness the rare battle of two species of the most ferocious ants in the United States.

Within half an hour an army of several thousand fire ants had massed and was charging back along the scent trail left by the scouts. As they approached the rabbit, they broke ranks and spread out to make a direct frontal attack on their enemies. They knew only too well that to enjoy the rabbit they would first have to fight for it.

143

The surprised Argentines were overwhelmed by the initial rush of the fiercely biting fire ants. Within minutes the rabbit had been overrun by fire ants, and the surviving Argentines had made a hasty retreat back toward their nest. Some of the more foolhardy elements of the fire ant army pursued the crippled Argentines for a considerable distance, then slowed and turned back toward the rabbit.

It was quite a distance back to the Argentine colony, so it took some time for the survivors of the attack to alert the colony. But when they did, it was a sight worth seeing. I have never seen so many angry ants in my life. It would have seemed that most of the colony's warriors were already out on the food trail, but now it looked as though they had been only a part of a population numbering in the tens of thousands. The army gathered the returning workers into its ranks and marched back along the trail to meet the fire ants.

By the time the Argentines approached the rabbit, it was almost covered with the formerly victorious fire ants. As the vengeance-seeking army approached, the fire ants took up the alarm and turned to meet their foe. Flushed with their easy victory, they seemed confident of success. The fire ants pouring down from the carcass were joined by hundreds of workers just arriving from their nest. In a sweeping mob they made their counterattack directly into the front ranks of the smaller, soft-bodied Argentines. As the first wave of fire ants struck the lead elements, the Argentines broke ranks at the point of attack and swallowed up the initial attackers by flowing out around them and attacking from the flank.

Surrounded by an obviously determined foe, the trapped fire ants panicked and tried to fight their way out of the shrinking circle of slashing jaws. In minutes they were overwhelmed and had disappeared beneath the platoons of warriors that attacked each fire ant. As individual warriors the Argentines would have been easily defeated by their stronger foe, but fighting in small platoons they quickly swallowed up the fire ants one at a time.

Now the main body of fire ants swept down upon the battleground. As they did, they were permitted to penetrate into the spreading wave of Argentines until the two armies seemed to have melted together.

battle between fire ants and Argentine ants

But the Argentines knew exactly what they were doing. They lost many warriors as the fire ants passed through, but then they formed platoons and buried individual fire ants. Antennae and legs were quickly and efficiently chopped off; then the heads of the now helpless fire ants were crushed before the platoons swept on to bury more victims.

Reinforcements arriving from the fire ant nest were not any more successful than the others had been. Long streams of Argentines were coming at them from every direction, breaking up the ranks of the fire ants and throwing them into panicked confusion. One fire ant warrior would be attacked and overthrown while his companion ignored him completely. But when an isolated Argentine was trapped, his fellow warriors would cut their way through to him. He might be dead before they reached him, but dozens of fire ants would be lying on the ground around him after his comrades were finished.

The tremendous battle lasted almost two hours before the surviving fire ants recognized the futility of continuing battle with their well-disciplined foe. Those who were able to run on the legs that they had left lost little time in getting away. It would take the fire ant nest at least another year to recover from its devastating losses.

There must have been thousands of dead and dying ants from both sides lying on the ground by the time the battle was over. Most of them were simply ignored by the victorious Argentines, though once in awhile one of them would drag a dead warrior back toward the nest. I didn't follow them long enough to find out what became of him.

Of course it wasn't long now before the Argentines turned back to stripping the rabbit. A nest the size of theirs needed as much food as the workers could supply. Unlike most other ants whose nests are at least partially limited by the life span of a single queen and by the number of eggs that she can lay in a lifetime, the Argentines are virtually un-limited. A nest may be as much as fifty years old and have countless thousands of ants. Such a nest may also contain dozens of egg-laying queens who have learned to live at peace with one another for the benefit of the colony.

The queens may mature at practically any time during the warm part of the year. Some of them will stay with the home colony, while

146

others will rebel at the crowded living conditions and will gather up a band of dissatisfied followers. With their small crowd of loyal workers, they will leave the main nest and build another colony nearby. As these neighboring colonies grow, they may gradually merge to produce an interconnecting network of thousands of tunnels and an unbelievably large nest.

The queens have wings like the queen ants of other species, but it is rare that a single queen will fly away to found a colony by herself. She is hardly larger than the workers and has no reserves of fat to last her until her first young are hatched out and able to help gather food for the colony. It is likely that they leave the home neighborhood only accidentally, having been blown away when they take flight above the nest during the swarming period when mating occurs. After this the queens lose their wings.

Except for the multi-queen organization of the nest, it is much like that of other ants. They build nurseries for their young, food storage chambers for the winter months, and large queen chambers for the egg-laying queens. Nurses care for the growing young while the warrior-workers defend the nest and forage for food.

Argentine ants setting out to find new nest

Hunting Guide

Scientific Names: (1) *Myrmeleon;* (2) *Iridomyrmex;* (3) *Solenopsis.*

Common Names: *Myrmeleon* is the ant lion, also known as the doodle bug.

Iridomyrmex is the Argentine ant.

Solenopsis is the fire ant.

ant lion adult *(myrmeleon)*

Description: The **ant lion** larva is a dirty grayish-brown color. It may be up to half an inch long and looks rather like a flat, hairy seed. The adult is from 1 to $1\frac{1}{2}$ inches long and looks very much like a damselfly except for the ant lion's promiment antennae with the enlarged tips.

The **Argentine ant** is about a tenth of an inch long and is colored brownish-black. It has a soft, easily damaged skeleton. The workers have no sting, but they have a poison-producing gland in the abdomen. The poison is often fatal to the small insects and larvae upon which they prey.

The reddish-brown **fire ant** is about two tenths of an inch long. These ants have gained quite a reputation for their ferocious tempers and painful stings. The effect of a quantity of these stings can be quite serious.

fire ant *(solenopsis)*

Habitat: The ant lion larva builds its nest in sheltered, sandy spots. The conical nests may often be found under old bridges or under overhanging rocks, where the sand will remain dry most of the year.

The Argentine ants build their nests in the ground, in woodpiles, in house foundations, and even in old tin cans. They are common throughout the Southland from the Atlantic to the Pacific.

148

The fire ants vary in color from a rather rare brownish-black to a much more common reddish-brown. The reddish-brown fire ants are about two-tenths of an inch long, while their darker colored relatives are slightly longer. But in one very important respect they are very much alike. They all have ferocious tempers and painful, often quite dangerous stings. Two or three stings can make a grown man ill, though in one instance a small boy received 250 stings on one side of his body—and he suffered no ill effects other than a very definite stinging sensation. He was a very tough little boy! The fire ants will attack anything that disturbs them. Within seconds after running up onto the intruder's body, they grasp his flesh with strong mandibles and almost immediately plunge their poisonous sting into the tiny fold of skin held by the mandibles. The area thus stung will turn red and white, swell, burn painfully for several minutes or longer, then start itching. Blisters will often form and later break open to produce irritating sores. Many victims of only a few of these stings will swell up so badly that they require medical treatment. It is little wonder that the fire ants fear few enemies other than the courageous little Argentine ants.

Stalking Methods: The ant lion larvae are perhaps the easiest to locate. Their nests are common in most sandy locations, especially if the area is sheltered. The adults are rarely found becauses of their short life span, but they may sometimes be taken with a sweep net in grasses on sandy soil.

Argentine ant *(iridomyrmex)*, worker

queen

winged male

149

The Argentine ants are such common pests in southern households and orchards that they are easily found. If they happen to be rare in your area, it may be helpful to set out baits of bread and honey to attract their scouts. The trail of workers can then be traced back to the colony.

The nests of the fire ants are easily recognizable. They range from about two or three inches to over a foot in height, and the base often measures two feet across. Single nests are more common in swamp-lands and wooded areas, while in the more favored open fields, there may be from forty to fifty nests per acre. Though the nests are usually built in the soil, on occasion they may be built in rotten stumps. Strangely enough, the best bait to attract these largely carnivorous ants is peanut butter. It has been found that four to six pounds per acre of poisoned peanut butter will completely eliminate all the fire ants in an infested area. Fortunately these hardy, ill-tempered ants are largely found only in the southeastern United States, though they have been reported as far west as Colorado. Wherever they occur, they are a serious threat both to man and to wild animals.

fire ant hills

13
Dragons and Crocodiles

The Flying Dragons

I used to think that dragons were either legendary creatures or that St. George had killed them all while rescuing fair maidens. Then several years ago I saw a flying dragon being born at the edge of a river at midnight. I have believed in them ever since.

I had been fishing in the river for several hours that night when my line got wrapped around a partially submerged stump about ten feet out from the shore. I pulled off my boots and was wading out toward the stump when a slimy, shadowy thing began crawling up out of the water and onto that same stump. Forgetting all about my fishing line, I backed out of the water much faster than I had gone into it.

A flashlight that I had in my tackle box didn't help much, though it did give me a better idea of the size of the thing. The creature had been trailing bits of moss and algae which reflected the pale moonlight to make it appear to be much larger than its two- or three-inch length. What it lacked in size it made up for in gruesome appearance. As the cold light from my flashlight struck ghostly fire from the huge, spherical eyes on the ugly head, the creature used its three pairs of spiny legs to drag itself slowly up onto the stump. Its upper body was heavily plated with armor, and its thrashing tail was long and scaly. It was not the sort of thing a lonely fisherman likes to meet at midnight.

When the thing had reached the top of the stump, it paused for a long while. By the time that I noticed that it was slowly swelling up, it quickly deflated itself back to its normal size. This was repeated several times until at last the armor plating on its back began to tear. Then there was another long pause. Finally the creature swelled up one last time and finished splitting the armor down the middle of its back.

Moving in slow motion as though each movement were painful, the glistening green creature within the torn armor began dragging itself out into the humid night air. First the ugly head was drawn out, then the lightly armored upper body, and finally the heavily spined legs. Long, glistening wings were folded and crumpled along the back, but as the creature emerged completely, the wings began to unfold.

Still in slow motion, the thing crawled over to the edge of the stump and lowered itself over the side. Hanging vertically now, it gradually pumped extra fluids into the wing veins until the wet, bedraggled wings had completely unfolded and were standing straight out from the body. There were two pairs of them, each pair about four inches across.

queen darner emerging

At last I recognized my green dragon. This was a big green darner, one of the largest and most ferocious dragonflies in the United States. This winged monster is one of the most aggressive meat-eating hunters of all of the insect swamplands and jungles. Few flying insects are safe from its swift attack. Its voracious appetite seldom permits it to rest.

It was getting late now. The first light of dawn was streaking the eastern sky, and the first of the hunting insects were already coming out of the swirling mists of the early morning. The clouds of mosquitoes were the worst of these so far as I was concerned.

The perching dragonfly peered intently into the air around his perch, stretched himself ever so slightly, then launched himself easily into the air on untried wings. Darting straight toward my head, he passed through one cloud of mosquitoes, snaring several of them in a spiny basket made by bunching up his six legs. The surprised victims were gobbled up in a matter of seconds; then the dragonfly was back for more. He stopped his raids on the mosquitoes only long enough to snare and kill a small robber fly that had been drawn to the riverbank by the blurred movements of the dragonfly. The poor robber fly had probably only intended to see what was going on, but he ended up as breakfast.

Other dragonflies were sweeping out over the river now, coming from their nightly resting places in the reeds and willows at the river's edge. I soon lost sight of my young dragon in the quick rush of dozens of pairs of glistening wings. It was difficult to see how any mosquitoes could survive such an attack by this squadron of dragons, but they manage.

Some of the dragonflies who were hunting over the river that morning had been born there and had only recently emerged from the muddy waters. But probably most of them had come there from other locations in search of a mate. Except at breeding times they often prefer to hunt far inland and may sometimes be seen darting about in mountain canyons in competition with the insect-hunting swifts and swallows who nest on the rocky cliffs. It is seldom that a dragonfly is taken by one of these hungry birds, though. The birds may be some of nature's best aerial acrobats, but they are no match for the elusive dragonfly who can fly forward at forty miles an hour, come to an abrupt halt, then fly backwards.

Some days I have even had various species of dragonflies follow me through dry pastures, swooping down to take the small insects that fly up at my approach. When I had a net with me, as I usually did, I would almost always try capturing one of these dragonflies on the wing. This was rarely successful. They always seemed to be just about two inches outside the net regardless of how fast or how careful I tried to be.

It is a simple matter to capture the dragonfly nymphs as compared to taking the swift adults. Many times I have pulled up cattails or other water plants growing at a pond's edge just to see how many different kinds of weird creatures I could find clinging among the roots. There were almost always one or more dragonfly nymphs squirming in the mud on the bottom of the plant.

Throughout the summer months you will see dragonflies darting back and forth over almost any farm pond, lake, or river. After mating in midair, the females will fly back and forth over the water until they find a spot that seems to satisfy them. Some species will drop down to deposit their eggs in crevices in various water grasses, but most of them prefer to fly along just above the surface of the water, dropping their eggs as they fly along. A few have adopted the dangerous practice of dipping the tip of the abdomen in the water so that the eggs will not float on top where they are likely to be eaten by minnows.

The long strings of eggs sink slowly to the ooze at the bottom where they usually go unnoticed by predatory insects and small fish. In a few days the warmth of the decaying organic material on the bottom causes them to hatch into the almost microscopic but already fierce young nymphs. At first the bloodthirsty little creatures have to be satisfied with meals of minute plants and animals known as plankton, but as they grow larger, they often take young minnows or even fingerling game fish.

In its year of underwater life the dragonfly nymph lives a leisurely life lying in ambush for the creatures unfortunate enough to swim within range of its peculiar jaws. When a water flea, a mayfly nymph, or a baby minnow comes close enough, the dragonfly nymph's hinged lower lip suddenly flips out for a distance of perhaps half an inch or more. Hooks on the end of the lip will tear into the victim's flesh as the nymph quickly draws its prey back into its powerful jaws. Within

154

minutes the victim is only a memory, and the little nymph is as hungry as ever.

Few of the nymphs will survive the entire year, and of these many will be killed as they perch wet and helpless at the water's edge early in the morning, having just crept out onto some log or reed to make the final change to adulthood. If the night is unusually damp, or if the emergence takes place only a short time before dawn, an early rising kingfisher or cuckoo may enjoy dragonfly steak for breakfast.

The Piranhas of the Insect Swamplands

Some of the more remote rivers of South America contain large schools of a bony little fish whose mouth seems to be filled with ragged teeth. These killer fish, known as piranhas, are so fast and use their teeth so efficiently that they can reduce a grown cow to a skeleton in about five minutes. Their attack is an unforgettable sight, one that would give you nightmares for years to come.

The one-to-two-inch long diving beetles of the North American ponds and lakes are the piranhas of the insect swamplands. Like the South American piranhas, they attack their prey with their powerful jaws. Unlike the piranhas, they also produce a very potent poison that can be released from the sides of their bodies to discourage their enemies. There is enough poison in one beetle to kill a young bullfrog.

So ferocious are the diving beetles and their meat-eating young that the larvae are called water tigers. Both the larvae and the adults feed on tadpoles, minnows, and aquatic insects. They dart through the water to plunge their jaws into the body of the victim, injecting it at the same time with a combination of digestive juices and deadly poison. The helpless victim will cease struggling within seconds, then slowly sink to the bottom as the beetle greedily sucks away its dissolving tissues.

Few are the intended victims that can escape these dread piranhas. The streamlined body of the beetle and its oarlike hind legs permit it to move through the water like a living torpedo, turning and twisting easily as its frantic victim vainly tries to escape.

Sometimes the beetle misjudges the size of its prey and may be drawn

down to the bottom of the pond where the struggles of its captive cause it to become entangled in the mat of decaying vegetation and slimy mud. If this happens, the beetle has only minutes of life left itself. It may be halfway through its meal when it realizes that its oxygen supply is almost gone. It must then struggle to escape the confining strands of grass. If it does not succeed, the struggle will become weaker and weaker and then cease altogether. The beetle's drowned body will soon become a part of the mud at the bottom.

Even the larvae must breathe air, though they spend their youth living in and under the water. Unlike the larvae of other aquatic insects, they are not equipped to breathe oxygen directly from the water. The adults have partially solved this problem with a sort of aqualungs. You may often see them resting near the surface of a pond with the tip of the abdomen sticking out of the water. They are gathering an air bubble between the wing covers and the abdomen, an air bubble that will gradually shrink as they use up the oxygen underwater.

In the breeding season, the female lays her thin-shelled, delicate eggs

156

predacious diving beetles hunting tadpoles

in slits cut into the leaves and stems of aquatic plants. Practically as soon as the eggs hatch, the young ones will begin attacking anything in sight, even attacking and killing one another if nothing more exciting comes their way. They will become adults within three weeks if a variety of food is readily available.

When the time comes for the change to adulthood, the larvae slowly drag themselves out of the water and crawl into the shelter of a damp rock or under an old log. Here each one will build a crude mud shelter within which it will gradually be transformed from a larva into a cocoon-encased pupa and finally into a very hungry adult.

The young adults are capable of living on land, and in fact they will often make long flying journeys overland at night. But their oar-like hind legs are designed for swimming and are clumsy on land.

Once in the water the clumsy beetle is so graceful that it is difficult to believe that it is the same creature.

In an aquarium these beetles are so active and so interesting that they make unusually exciting specimens. The only problem is that nothing else can live in the aquarium with them, or at least not for long. If they run out of fresh meat, they may kill and eat one another. They might try to make a meal out of you if you stick your finger in the water. They may be smaller than the South American piranhas, but they make up for it with their fierce appetites. Even a young piranha would probably be considered a tasty treat to the adult diving beetle.

The Flying Crocodiles

Perhaps the most dangerous of the many different insect crocodiles is the two-inch-long killer known as the giant water bug. The first ones that I ever saw were crawling along the main street of a small town about nine o'clock at night. The street was speckled with the yellow glow of lighted store windows to which thousands of insects had been attracted that summer night. The giant water bugs were flat-bodied, brown insects with strange legs. The front pair of legs were curved around in front of the broad and slightly elongate head, while the hind legs looked as though they were better suited for swimming than for crawling down a city street.

The big bugs looked so odd that I foolishly picked one up, intending to keep it for observation in an aquarium. That was a mistake I have never made since. I had no sooner lifted it than it grabbed my hand with its sharp forelegs, then plunged its poisonous beak into me to give the most unbelievably painful bite I have ever experienced. My whole hand felt as if it were on fire. The worst part of all was that the thing didn't want to let go of me. I had to literally tear it off of my bleeding hand. From that time on I have been more careful about picking up unfamiliar insects with my bare hands.

It was not too long after this that I discovered several of these giant bugs in a goldfish pond on a college campus near my home. They couldn't have been there for very many days, or there wouldn't have been any goldfish left. I spent almost one entire afternoon sitting on the edge of the pond watching the dangerous hunters work.

Most of the goldfish in the pond were five or six inches long, but there were a few younger ones who ranged in size from about two to

158

three or four inches and these young ones had been attacked by the water bugs. I could see the remains of at least one or two victims lying on the murky bottom of the concrete pool.

One goldfish is more than enough of a meal for quite some time, so the water bugs were not continuously chasing their captive prey. While I was there that afternoon, only two goldfish were attacked. The first one was a fairly large one, larger than the water bug that attacked it.

At first the water bug made several feints at the fish which easily eluded him. Then he became more serious and darted through the water after his victim. The terrified goldfish was so fast and elusive that the water bug was having a very difficult time. To add to his difficulties, one of the largest goldfish darted into him and grabbed him by one hind leg. As quickly as the water bug turned to try to bite his tormentor, the big fish spit him out and shot out of range with a flick of his tail.

The water bug didn't give up easily, though. He selected another, smaller victim and quickly drew up alongside it despite the fish's evasive tactics. As he came within reach of his victim, his barbed fore-leg shot out, and he clamped onto the fish's scaly side. In an instant he had plunged his curved beak into his captive and injected his poison. The fish went wild at that, twisting and leaping out of the water in a frantic effort to rid itself of its attacker.

Instead of trying to help, the other goldfish became alarmed and swam to the other end of the pool. There was not really anything they could do, anyway. The poison worked quickly, and the fish was soon drifting slowly toward the bottom with its attacker riding it down and feeding all the time.

I came back later that afternoon with a net and was removing the destructive beetles to a water-filled gallon pickle jar when one of the school officials came running out with a horrified expression. At first he thought I was stealing the goldfish, but he was equally indignant when he found out that I was removing the water bugs. He gave me a stern lecture on the preservation of all nature's wild creatures, and I gave him a giant water bug. A few minutes later he was fishing out the rest of the bugs for me.

159

giant water bug killing goldfish

In most ponds and lakes the giant water bugs hide among the tangled weeds near the shore. When a frog, snake, or small fish comes within range, they make a sudden dart and pounce onto the hapless victim before it can make a move to defend itself. Once the water bug is firmly attached, its victim is as good as dead. It takes only a fraction of a second to drive the paralyzing poison into the victim's flesh.

If there is anything more fierce than a male water bug, it is a female water bug. Most insect females are the dominant members of the species, but the female of one species of water bug overdoes it. When she is ready to lay her eggs, she seizes the poor male and ejects a water-proof glue onto his back. Into this she embeds her hundred or more eggs and thus forces the male to baby-sit until the eggs hatch. She could hardly find a safer spot for them.

Hunting Guide

Scientific Names: (1) *Anax;* (2) *Dysticus;* (3) *Lethocerus;* (4) *Belostoma;* (5) *Abedus.*

Common Names: *Anax* is the dragonfly, also known as the giant green darner, mosquito hawk, darning needle, snake feeder, snake doctor, and horse stinger.

Dysticus is known as the predacious diving beetle. The larvae are called water tigers.

Lethocerus is commonly known as the giant water bug and as the electric light bug. *Belostoma* and *Abedus* are smaller members of the giant water bug family.

Description: The **giant green darner** is about three inches long and has a four-inch wingspread. The transparent wings are criss-crossed with a network of yellowish-brown veins. The thorax is a greenish color, and the abdomen is blue-green.

queen darner larva

161

"water tiger"
(larva of predacious diving beetle)

giant water bug with eggs

The **predacious diving beetle** is over one inch long. It is an oval, flattened beetle with a very dark brown to black colored body. It may be recognized in the water by its oarlike hind legs and by the breast stroke which it uses for swimming.

The **giant water bug** is a large, flat, brown bug with its middle and hind legs designed for swimming. The front pair of legs is designed like tongs. The broad head is slightly extended beneath the eyes. The adults range from one to two inches in length, depending upon the species.

Habitat: The big green darner is common around weedy ponds and may occasionally be found in pastures from April to October.

The predacious diving beetle is common in stagnant ponds, in streams, and along the edges of lakes and sluggish rivers.

The giant water bug is commonly found in pools filled with vegetation such as cattails and sedges.

Stalking Methods: The big green darner should be hunted with a lightweight, flexible net in pastures with tall grass, and along the edges of ponds and lakes. They may be most easily captured while they are perched on a weed stem or on an old stump or log.

The diving beetles and giant water bugs may be taken by sweeping a dip net through vegetation at the edge of a pond or stream. They may also be taken at lights at night, provided that there is a pond or lake nearby. The diving beetles may occasionally be taken at lights far from water, for they are great overland travelers.

14
Drinkers of Nectar, Makers of Honey

The common little honeybee is largely responsible for the fact that the United States is able to produce such huge surpluses of food every year. Without the aid of the honeybees it is quite likely that many Americans would be going hungry and that the price of food would be doubled. It may sound fantastic that many important food crops depend on honeybees for up to eighty percent of their pollination, but this is only because we take such things for granted. In areas where insecticides were once carelessly handled, farmers quickly learned their lessons. In some such instances honeybees had to be imported to prevent expensive crop losses.

Some commercial beekeepers show their appreciation to the honeybees by giving them a winter home in California and by sending them to the cooler mountain country of Utah to spend the summer. It takes 100 to 150 large trucks to carry all the high-living California bees to Utah each spring. The farmers in Utah will even provide fresh honey for the bees when they are unable to make enough for themselves. Ridiculous? Not at all. There are thirty thousand acres of commercially grown alfalfa in Utah, a crop that would be worth only about one-third as much without the pollination service provided by the pampered California bees.

Unfortunately for the bees, alfalfa produces such small amounts of nectar that it is often not possible for the bees to produce enough honey to feed the hive. In that case, the farmers will gladly provide all the honey that the bees need for the summer. If anything happened to these bees, the poor alfalfa crops that year might ruin the farmer financially.

In years of severe drought, pollen production is so poor in some parts of the country that beekeepers must have pollen shipped to them from the South where the mild winters permit the bees to gather extra pollen all through the winter. Nevertheless, most bees still have to work pretty hard for their living. One pound of honey that sells for less than a dollar in the grocery store required up to thirty-seven thousand flights that may have covered over fifty thousand miles. This is roughly equivalent to five round trips from New York City to Los Angeles. Where else can you find any creatures who will do so much work without pay to produce less than a dollar's worth of goods? It requires a single bee about thirty minutes to gather one drop of nectar and a load of pollen. The drop of nectar doesn't become honey until most of it has evaporated.

honeybees on alfalfa

When you have a free summer afternoon, try setting out a dish of honeycomb dripping with honey. It would be best to put it out in a patch of white clover or near some flowering fruit trees to which honeybees are attracted. The bees will ignore the honey for a long time, but finally an adventurous worker or a scout bee will discover the dish. After a single bee has visited it and has drunk her fill, it will usually be only a matter of minutes before there will be a steady stream of bees coming directly from the hive to the saucer and back again.

Now if it takes so long for one single bee to find the honey, why do so many bees suddenly begin coming to the dish? Bees can neither talk nor make any sort of sound that would tell their fellow workers about the find. In fact the scout who discovered the treasure may not even return to it! Her work is done. She will be more concerned with finding other good harvest areas.

For centuries beekeepers have been puzzled over how all the bees in a hive can be told about the location of a new crop of flowers or an orchard that has just begun to bloom. The only thing that they could be sure of was that the bees were not talking.

It had long been known that certain bees returning to a hive would be more excited than the others. These excited workers would run about over the honeycomb in what appeared to be a frenzied dance. Other bees would gather about the dancers, whom they could smell and feel but not see in the dark hive. Soon others would be joining in the dance. After a few minutes a large flight of bees would leave the hive and fly directly to a new source of food.

Eventually a professor at the University of Munich was able to break the secret code of the bees. Dr. Karl von Frisch was able to interpret the dance of the bees in terms of actual locations of fields and orchards. A circular dance indicated a nearby food source, while a figure-eight dance indicated that the food was as much as three miles away. The direction in which the figure eight was formed indicated the direction of the food. A peculiar wagging of the scout's tail told the bees almost the exact distance between the hive and the food—the faster the tail, the farther away the food.

165

A similar dance is performed when a swarm leaves the hive. This takes place most commonly in late spring or early summer when flowers are most plentiful. A short time before the hive gives off a swarm, the foraging bees will become lazy and stop gathering food. Some of them will begin making exploratory flights to find possible hive-building sites.

Within a day or two the old queen will leave the hive with a cloud of loyal followers. They will fly a short distance to a preselected, temporary resting place where the swarm will surround the queen. From here there will be scouts flying off to study the proposed new homesites. Each scout will return after a time to give her opinion of the site she has visited. The better the site, the more enthusiastic will her dance be.

When the choice has been narrowed down, most of the scouts will visit the favored sites, then help the swarm decide on the best one. When they all agree, the swarm moves to the chosen spot and immediately begins to construct a comb within which the queen can lay her eggs. As the comb grows, cells in the back and upper part of it will be used for storage of nectar and pollen. Beekeepers take advantage of this storage habit of their bees by putting harvest combs in the top of the hive. This way they do not have any problems with bee larvae getting into the honey they sell. The larvae may be clean and harmless, but who wants to eat them?

Like the bumblebee, the honeybees produce a waxy secretion from between the segments of the abdomen. This soft wax is removed with the mandibles and used to build the waxen cells of which the comb is constructed. When the rough cell has been completed, nurse bees will varnish the inside by thoroughly licking the wax lining. Until this is done, the queen would not think of laying an egg inside it.

There is probably no difference between any of the fertilized eggs that the queen lays; yet some of them will produce queens, while the majority of them will produce only the smaller workers. The difference is believed to be due to selective feeding of the larvae. Those destined to become queens will be fed larger quantities of nectar and pollen, and in addition the nurse bees will feed them with generous amounts of royal jelly. This mysterious jelly is produced by glands in the nurse bee's head. Probably all the larvae receive some of this, but the queen

166

bee larvae receive far more of it than do the others. At one time this royal jelly was selling at very high prices because some people believed that it would keep them from growing old. As they eventually found out, it works much better if you happen to be a bee larva.

The eggs that the queen lays will hatch into little white grubs or larvae in about three days. For the first six days of its life the helpless larva will eat almost constantly and will grow so fast that you can almost see it increasing in size. Then all of a sudden the larva loses its appetite and goes to sleep. Its cell will then be carefully sealed by a nurse bee so that its rest will not be disturbed. Twelve days later a young adult will emerge. For awhile she will be so weak that she must be fed by other workers before she will have enough energy to move about the hive.

The first three weeks of the worker's life are spent in the hive where she serves as a housekeeper, nursemaid, and guard. By the fourth week she is ready to leave the hive for the first time, though she may have spent several days flying around near the hive in order to memorize its location. For the next three weeks she will make continuous flights afield unless she falls victim to a robber fly, dragonfly, bee wolf, or insecticide.

Occasionally a bee will bring back a load of nectar and pollen that has been poisoned with insecticide. If very many bees are visiting the poisoned flowers, they will bring back enough to poison fifty or so pounds of stored honey in the hive. Yet poisoned honey has never been a problem in spite of sometimes heavy losses of foraging bees from poisoned flowers. What protects the honey? The answer is quite surprising. When a returning worker arrives at the hive with nectar and pollen, she will transfer it to other bees working in the hive. These workers will then pass it on to still more workers until dozens of bees will be involved in the transfer. If the nectar is poisoned, it will sicken each of the workers who carries it. Since a sick bee will immediately leave the hive, all the poisoned nectar will be carried away from the hive with the dying workers.

In addition to predators and poisons, the bees in such complicated living quarters will have many more problems that must be solved.

167

Sometimes in the middle of the summer the hive will become hot and dry, making a very dangerous climate for the soft-bodied larvae who will quickly dry out unless something is done. To solve this problem, the nurse bees and other young workers in the hive will refuse to accept nectar from the returning bees, but they will eagerly welcome those few bees who are bringing in fresh water. The other workers quickly get the idea and begin bringing in loads of water. The hive bees smear the water over the comb, then evaporate it by rapidly beating their wings. This unique air conditioning system does the job very nicely.

Of course when you have thousands of bees bringing in drops of water, you could expect the hive to be flooded in a short time. How do the hive bees prevent this? They simply ignore the water-carrying workers when they have enough to get the job done. The confused workers find that only the nectar bearers are welcome, so it's off to the flowers again.

It would be difficult to imagine how even the ingenious bees can survive the intense cold in the northern states. Not all honeybees are fortunate enough to have a winter home in California. Those who do not live in warm climates have used some characteristic American know-how to solve their problems. They gather into a huge living ball on top of a honey-storage comb. The bees at the inside of the ball will eat their fill while being warmed by the mass of their fellow workers fighting for a position on the comb. As the struggle continues, the bees on the inside of the ball are constantly being pushed outside, and those on the outside are working their way inside. The activity and the energy-producing honey both help to keep them all quite comfortable no matter how cold it gets outside.

The worker honeybee's 160 to 220 wingbeats per second require very large amounts of energy, especially for flights of up to four miles. If the bee was a meat-eater, it is unlikely that she could work half as hard. As any good athlete knows, simple sugars such as glucose are rapidly utilized for extra enegry, while fats and protein in meat are good body builders, but are only slowly utilized as a source of energy. Since it is not possible for the bee to store enough sugar in her muscles to maintain herself for long flights, she makes use of an auxiliary

168

interior of beehive showing queen's cell at bottom

fuel tank called the honey crop, or honey stomach. She can carry enough honey or nectar in this extra stomach to keep her going a long while.

In warm, windy weather the evaporation of water from flowers will concentrate the nectar so much that it may be as much as forty percent sugar. It seldom gets above this concentration because the bees will drain the flower dry by this time. On humid days and in the early morning, the sugar content may be as little as ten to sixteen percent. Since seventy to eighty percent of honey is made up of various sugars, you can see that the bees have to work only a fourth as hard to gather the same amount of sugar during the middle of a dry day as they will during a humid morning. But instead of slowing down in times of plenty, the bees simply take advantage of their opportunity to produce much larger quantities of honey in a short time.

The hard-working bees apparently do not really intend to bring back pollen with their load of nectar, but they can't help themselves. The thick hairs on the hind legs form a natural trap for the sticky pollen. By the time the bee has visited several dozen flowers on a single trip, the so-called pollen basket made of the hairs on the legs will have picked up a full load of pollen which will be removed by other workers waiting at the hive. This seemingly accidental gathering of pollen provides the bees with necessary proteins, fats, and minerals while at the same time it ensures cross-pollination of the flowers that were visited. Since many plants will not produce their fruit without cross-pollination either by wind or by insects, you can see that the bee is also providing food for man both as honey and in the form of improved crops. Can you think of a single animal that works harder or does more to help feed mankind? Thank goodness for the honeybee's hairy hind legs.

Hunting Guide
Scientific Name: *Apis*.

Common Name: This is the honeybee, also known as the hive bee and simply as the bee. It is only one of more than three

honeybee *(apis)*

thousand different species of bees in the United States.

Description: The adult female worker of the honeybee in the United States is to be golden-brown thorax is covered with thick bristles. The rear edge of each of the golden-brown segments of the less bristly abdomen is marked with a band of dark brown.

Habitat: Almost every colony of the domestic honeybee in the United States is to be found in a hive built by a beekeeper. The rare wild colony in sparsely populated, forested country was in every instance started by a swarm of honeybees who originally escaped from an apiary. The honeybee that we know was imported into New England sometime around the year 1638, so it is not surprising that we can read of instances in which pioneer families robbed "wild bee" trees. Nevertheless, these so-called wild bees were all descendants of the domesticated colonies brought to America in the seventeenth century.

Stalking Methods: It is disappointing but true that you can most easily locate bee hives in your neighborhood (within two or three miles of your home) by looking up "Beekeepers" in the Yellow Pages of your telephone directory. The advantage of this particular hunting method is that a friendly beekeeper may be willing to show you his hives and explain something about his method for gathering honey. On the other hand you may prefer to track down the hive yourself on the chance that it will be a wild one in some brushy vacant

queen

drone

worker

171

lot or in a woody area in your nearest city park. In this case you should first set out a bait of honey and honeycomb in an area frequented by honeybees. You will find that the bees will fly in almost a straight line from the bait to the hive, though there will always be some random flying around the bait before they settle down. By standing well back from the honeycomb, you should be able to determine the direction that is being taken. When you have this, carefully indicate the direction of flight by drawing a corresponding straight line on a map of your part of the city. Now go to another location about three or four hundred yards to one side of the line of flight and again set out your bait. Draw a line on your map to indicate the direction in which your newly attracted bees are flying. You will probably find that the two lines will cross at some point within two miles of your home. You should make several different sightings from different locations, setting out bait in many places around the hive so that your lines on the map look like the spokes of a wheel with the hive right in the center.

mapping to locate beehive

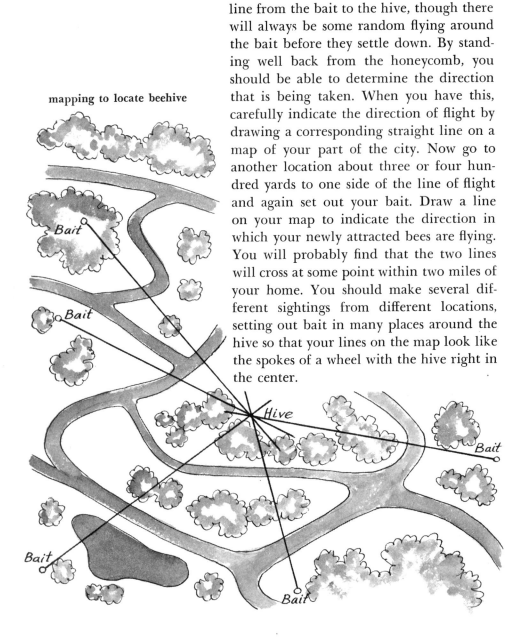

15
Tropical Birds
of the Insect Jungles

Migration of the Flowers

As the frosted fingertips of winter begin probing down into the wilderness of northern Canada, isolated pairs of Canada geese will gather together for their annual southward flight. Sometime in the late autumn you will hear their calls high and mournful as they fly through the moonlit sky on their way to the Gulf of Mexico. Have you ever considered how remarkable it is that even these powerful birds are able to travel over two thousand miles in the space of a few weeks? Yet the golden brown monarch butterfly makes this same trip on a pair of wings as fragile as tissue paper.

You may think that the monarchs find the trip far less hazardous than the much hunted geese, but the weary butterflies have troubles of their own. Their migratory trips will often take them through territory claimed by other species of butterflies as their own. Whenever this happens, the innocent monarchs will be attacked and chased from the flowers upon which they try to feed.

I had never known that butterflies could be so hot-tempered until the day a red admiral butterfly in my backward made a fierce, dive-bombing attack on a monarch who was apparently just passing through. The monarch was carelessly sailing along about three or four feet above the ground when the red admiral pounced on him without warning. The startled monarch instantly slipped sideways and took evasive action, but the angry red admiral was not about to let him get away so easily. Whenever the monarch tried to gain altitude for maneuvering, the red admiral would dart around him in dizzying circles, then rise above the monarch and swoop down at his head. Finally the confused monarch must have reached the boundary of the territory of the red

173

admiral because his opponent suddenly lost all interest in him and went back to feeding peaceably on the flowers along my fence.

The monarchs passing through my neighborhood seemed to be having an unusually hard time that year. Not too long after the red admiral incident, two monarchs happened to pass over my elm trees while I had my trained Harris hawk out in the yard with me. My hawk had made half a dozen short flights from her perch to my fist when the monarchs caught her eye. In order to get a better look at the strangers, she twisted her neck until her head was almost upside down, then snapped upright and leaped off the perch.

The poor monarchs never had a chance. The first one was snatched out of the air with one foot and crammed into the hawk's beak as she plunged toward the other one. In less than three minutes the big bird was dropping back toward her perch while fragments of golden-brown wings drifted toward the grass.

I had heard of hawks attacking monarchs in flight, but this was the first time I ever believed it. Most birds with any sense will leave the foul-tasting monarchs alone, but hawks have never been noted for their sense of taste. Occasionally a young woodpecker or flicker will

red admiral chasing monarch butterfly

swoop down and grab a resting monarch, but the butterfly's tough skin will protect him until he has a chance to exude some unbelievably bad-tasting fluid from glands in the side of his body. One taste is enough for a lifetime. That bird will never again touch a monarch butterfly. I will never know if my hawk had learned this lesson. Those were the last monarchs she saw before I released her in the fall of the year.

The monarchs were far more plentiful in the following year. A mild, humid spring had encouraged both egg laying and early emergence of the first caterpillars of the year. Soon the young butterflies as well as some of the survivors of the past year's migration were winging their way northward. By early June there were small flights moving across the milkweed-infested pastures of Kansas and Missouri, stopping only long enough to lay their eggs and make a few visits to the wild flowers in those same fields.

The egg-laying females were careless at that time of the year, so I had expected it to be a simple matter to approach them as they laid their eggs on the milkweed leaves. One morning in the last week of June I stationed myself near some of these plants in a nearby park. I must have waited there for several hours without any success. The thick grass and scattered wild flowers were swarming with many different kinds of insects, but there was no sign of the monarchs. It was not until early that afternoon that a single monarch fluttered over the tops of some nearby oak trees and glided unsteadily down to the milk-weed patch.

This first monarch was soon followed by several others, only one of which stopped long enough to lay some of her several hundred eggs. This little female investigated one plant after another before finally approving of one. She alighted on one of the topmost leaves of the selected plant and curled her abdomen beneath the leaf. A moment later she fluttered away to another plant and repeated this process. Each time she alighted, she left a shiny, jade-green egg about the size of a large dew drop. Each of the fragile looking little eggs was covered with an unusually tough shell.

For the next four days I visited the egg-bearing plants daily. By the fourth day only a fragment remained of one of the eggs, the shell having been eaten by the hungry little black, gold, and white-striped caterpillar who had hatched before I arrived that morning. The other egg appeared lifeless, but by late in the morning a tiny caterpillar was crawling out of it onto the leaf on which it would soon begin feeding.

It did not take long for the first two hungry caterpillars to begin shredding the milkweed leaves. They ate almost constantly, pausing only for short periods of rest or to molt the old skins that were becoming too tight for their growing bodies.

No one is quite certain why the monarchs prefer milkweed to any other plant. The young ones will starve to death if they cannot have milkweed leaves to eat. Monarchs that have traveled to Europe on everything from tramp freighters to luxury liners are so rare that they are highly prized as collector's items. These butterflies are established in Asia and Australia. Probably the only reason that they have not spread to Europe is because of the lack of milkweed plants there, and the monarch flatly refuses to lay her eggs anywhere else.

My caterpillars roamed freely from one milkweed plant to another during their week in the larval stage. They never showed an interest in any other plants regardless of how tender or juicy the leaves might have been. The only time they would ever consider abandoning the milkweed is when it comes time to spin a cocoon.

By the end of the week I had lost track of the first two caterpillars as others emerged and began feeding, but I did have the opportunity to watch one large monarch caterpillar preparing for adulthood. When I found it, this particular caterpillar was laboriously inching up the side of a walnut tree until it came to a spindly branch about seven or eight feet above the ground. It crawled out on the branch, investigated several leaves and twigs, then crawled down under a twig near the end of the branch. It rested there for a few minutes, then glued its tail to the twig with a dab of silk from the tip of its abdomen. As the sticky material hardened in the hot summer air, the caterpillar let go of the twig and hung head downwards.

I knew that the old skin would have to be shed before the cocoon could be formed, but it was an hour or more before anything happened. Finally the muscles began twitching in the caterpillar's body as little

176

ripples of movement started near the head and spread in waves down the caterpillar's back. The dry outer skin soon split, and the caterpillar began squirming and twisting about in it like a big man trying to get out of a small raincoat.

Soon the old skin fell to the ground, and the caterpillar was able to start forming its shiny green cocoon, better known as a pupal case or chrysalis. This begins as a soft, sticky green coating that covers the caterpillar's entire body. This coating slowly thickens and then dries out over a period of a day or two. I knew that the process would be slow and uninteresting for several hours, so I left my caterpillar alone for the rest of the day.

When I returned the following morning, the sticky green mess had become a jade-green chrysalis decorated with a thin black line and with dots of shining gold crystals. The case was now hard and waxy.

During the following week the chrysalis gradually changed in color as the body of the growing adult within began showing through the translucent covering. By the end of the week the deep green, inch-long chrysalis had become dark brown along the sides where the wings were forming. This soon changed to a bluish-black as the time for emergence neared. On the last day before the emergence, the chrysalis faded and gradually became almost transparent along its lower half while a frosty coating appeared on the upper part.

I was late arriving the next day, and the wet butterfly had already emerged. The monarch was still too damp and limp to think about flying, but she was already making her preparations. She was pumping fluids through the heavy wing veins, blowing them up until they stiffened and forced the crumpled wings to unfold. A slight breeze rippling through the leaves helped the drying process enough that in less than an hour after her emergence the monarch was able to flutter away.

That particular monarch may have reached the wilds of northern Canada, but she was one of the lucky few if she did. Only one out of two or three hundred butterflies ever lives to see that country. Most of the monarchs who do reach Canada are the children or the grandchildren of the migrants who started out from the southland in the spring.

177

The survivors of the perilous northward journey and the far greater numbers of their Canadian-born descendants will begin another migration early the next autumn. This time they are headed south, sometimes traveling in flocks of several million individuals.

Before the first hard frosts in Canada kill the remaining eggs and caterpillars, the migrating adults will be arriving in winter homes from Florida to California. A few of the hardier ones will even fly down to Argentina for the winter.

In Pacific Grove, California, the world's only refuge for butterflies has been established by law. Here the monarchs come by the millions each fall, returning to roost in the same trees year after year. The butterfly trees, as they are called, are so weighted down with the monarchs that it seems a wonder that the weaker limbs do not break under their burden. Yet there will be identical trees right around them in which few or no butterflies will be roosting. Why the butterflies prefer one tree to another is still a mystery. The thing that makes it even more of a mystery is the fact that the largest number of these butterflies are newcomers who have never seen that tree before now and will probably never see it again.

The butterflies roosting in the California butterfly trees will remain largely dormant for the winter, arousing only long enough to make brief visits to flowers in the surrounding fields. But in Florida and Mexico the monarchs remain more active and will usually breed and lay eggs all during the winter. By the following spring there will be far more migrants heading northward than there were arriving in the southland the year before.

Except for the hazards on the migration, the monarchs enjoy a carefree life. All they require is sunshine, a few flowers, and milkweed. Their needs are simple, and so are their troubles.

Furry Green Fairies Who Fly by Moonlight

I remember that when I was about five or six years old the darkness around my grandmother's country home was often so complete that it was impossible to see at night unless the moon was out. One night I

migrating monarchs resting
in California pepper tree

was out with a cousin about my same age making a trip of about half a mile down a dark country road to get home from a neighbor's farm. That was undoubtedly the blackest night we ever saw. By the time we reached my grandmother's house we were getting pretty nervous.

Grandmother laughed at our fears and told us that a night such as this one brings out some of the most unusual and beautiful living creatures in the world. She had showed us some night-blooming moon-flowers before this, and we thought that was what she meant. When she went on to explain about the furry green fairies who come out in the dark of night, we were all ears.

That night Grandmother showed us how to make the magic potion that would bring the delicate little creatures to our own yard. First she mixed a bit of yeast into some honey, then mashed some overripe bananas into the sticky mess. This was thinned slightly with water, then allowed to sit undisturbed in a crockery bowl for the next two or three days.

Just about the time my cousin and I were ready to give up on waiting for the potion to ripen, Grandmother called us into the house and gave each of us a small jar of the sweetish, bubbling liquid. We were in-structed to smear generous amounts of this gooey syrup on some apple trees behind the house. My cousin and I looked at each other with blank expressions, then went ahead and followed Grandmother's instructions. We couldn't help thinking that she must be playing some kind of trick on us.

By ten o'clock that night, when my cousin and I were both so sleepy that we could hardly sit up straight, Grandmother took us out to the apple trees. She was carrying a flashlight which she didn't use until we had approached the first tree. When she switched the light on, there were several little grayish-brown moths around the syrup but nothing else. Now we were sure that Grandmother had just played a joke on us.

The second tree was not any more rewarding, but at the third tree we really got the shock of our lives! There was the most beautiful winged creature resting there that either of us had ever seen. Its wing-spread was about four inches, but its short, furry body was not more than 1½ inches long. A long, green tail curved gracefully down from

180

behind each wing. Each of the pale green wings was bordered along the front edge with a streak of purple, and each wing was decorated with an eyelike spot.

luna moth (*actias*)

As we watched the delicate creature breathlessly, a second and then a third of these furry green luna moths settled down upon the tree with gently quivering wings. One of them remained only a moment, then flew over to the light in Grandmother's hand. Grandmother immediately switched off the flashlight, and the shadowy moth fluttered back to the tree.

We would have captured at least one of the beautiful insect fairies that night, but Grandmother gently persuaded us to leave them unharmed. Though that was many years ago, I am still glad that we did not bother the little fairies that night. We would have lost much more than we would have gained, though years had to pass before I understood why that would be so.

Hunting Guide

Scientific Names: (1) *Danaus;* (2) *Actias.*

Common Names: *Danaus* is the monarch butterfly, also known by the names of milkweed butterfly and storm fritillary.

Actias is the luna moth.

Description: The **monarch** has a 3½- to 4-inch wingspread. The golden-brown wings are crisscrossed with black veins. Each segment of the body bears black and yellow stripes. The larvae (caterpillars) are strikingly marked with bands of white, black, and gold.

The **luna moth** is a graceful, furry green moth with a wingspread of about four inches. The rear of each wing is drawn out into a long, tail-like appendage. The front of each wing is topped by a purple border, beneath which is a spot resembling an eye. The larva of the luna moth is a bright, glassy green with a yellow line along each side.

monarch cocoon

182

Habitat: The monarch is found from Canada to South America, most frequently around fields of milkweed, goldenrod, thistles, red clover, asters, and butterfly weed. The larvae will be found almost exclusively on milkweed.

The luna moth may be found east of the Rocky Mountains, from Canada to the Gulf of Mexico. These moths are most easily found in the vicinity of walnut, birch, beech, willow, oak, and hickory trees because these are the leaves on which the larvae feed, and this is where the eggs are laid. The adults may be attracted at night to fruit trees where they may obtain sweet sap from injured trees as well as from the fermented fruit on the ground.

Stalking Methods: Monarchs may be found all through the summer and early autumn visiting cultivated flower beds as well as clover and other wild flowers in fields and at the edges of highways. They are easiest to net during the spring and late autumn. A captured monarch may sometimes fall on its side and pretend to be dead. When they do that, I am usually tempted to release the little fakers. The butterflies may be raised from chrysalises collected from milkweed plants. For the best results, the chrysalises should be kept in a lightly moistened, well-ventilated cage.

The luna moth remains hidden during the day, and it is extremely difficult to spot then. At night they may be rather easily taken around outdoor lights, or at trees baited with fermented honey and bananas.

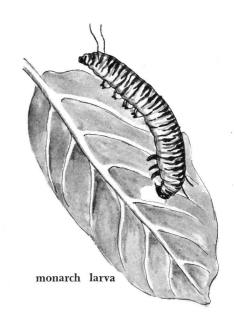

monarch larva

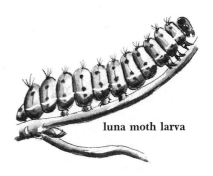

luna moth larva

183

16
Stalking and Trapping Big Game Insects

It is a fine midsummer day, and I would like to have you come along with me on a collecting trip into the wilderness of a city park. You make the captures, and I'll carry enough collecting equipment to give me an excuse to stay out of your way. When my feet begin dragging long furrows in the grass by the end of the day, you will see why I have suggested that you carry only a small amount of collecting equipment. It gets heavy after two or three hours.

The park in which we are going to hunt is a rambling, partially wooded area of about one hundred acres. We will cross open grasslands first then enter a thicket of sumac and oak saplings. On the other side of the tangled thicket there is a small lake with numerous cattails growing along the marshy edge.

As we enter the open grasslands, you will need one of the three different nets that I carry. This first net will be a heavy beating net, so called because you actually beat bushes and grass clumps with it.

The grass where we are standing is as much as two feet tall in places. Here you vigorously swing your beating net back and forth through the thick grass. After about half a dozen sweeps you stop and discover dozens of insects of every size and description running, hopping, and crawling around inside the heavy cloth bag that forms the net. There are grasshoppers of course, several crickets, a robber fly, some tiny beetles, a few ants, and many others that we do not recognize.

If you want to keep some of these specimens for your insect zoo, I will give you a glass fruit jar with a wire screen top. We have several of these collecting jars, each of which is stuffed about half full with well-dried grass. This helps to keep the insects from becoming too crowded and discourages them from fighting with one another.

For those insects that you want to mount in your insect collection, you will need a killing jar containing a wad of cotton moistened with a little benzene which you can buy from any drugstore. We have used a piece of cardboard to cover the cotton so that the insects will not get their feet tangled in the cotton fibers.

As we get halfway over the grassland, we see clover, buttercups, thistles, and milkweed growing in scattered patches in the dry soil. These are worth investigating. Carefully we stalk the flowers in search of honeybees, tiny solitary bees, miniature wasps, and butterflies. Inside of one buttercup we find a sleeping firefly which we leave in peace. Before we can move on, a white cabbage butterfly flutters down onto a clover blossom directly in front of us. This one will not be taken with the beating net because the heavy bag might crush its delicate wings. Instead, I give you the lightweight butterfly net made with a deep bag of minnow seine netting bought from a sporting goods store.

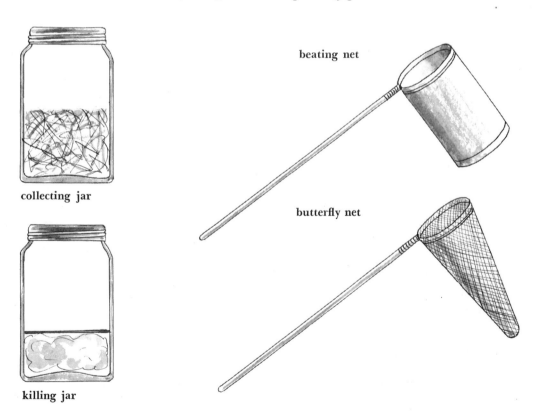

collecting jar

killing jar

beating net

butterfly net

To capture the butterfly you must make a quick sideways sweep, then twist the net halfway over right after the capture. This causes the bag to fall over the hoop and thus imprisons the startled little creature.

Gently now we remove the butterfly with tweezers and put it into a killing jar that is reserved for butterflies and moths only. If we put beetles, robber flies, or grasshoppers in the same jar, they would get covered with the bright scales of the butterflies who had been in the jar previously. In a few minutes the little butterfly stops struggling and falls to the cardboard at the bottom of the jar. We will let it remain there for several more minutes before putting it into a dry grass-lined box. To avoid rubbing off any of its scales, we must handle it by one leg with a pair of tweezers.

tweezers holding butterfly

As we walk along through the grass, we see butterflies of many different species. We are fortunate that this is a clear, warm day with very little wind. This is the best time for butterfly hunting because they do not like to fly on cool, cloudy, or windy days. There will be quite a variety out in this open field, but we could also find some interesting woodland specimens in the weeds bordering the woods on the right-hand side of the park. We may also find them sipping water from a mud puddle formed by a recent thunderstorm.

If we lie down in the grass near a patch of wild flowers, we may soon be able to watch a robber fly pouncing upon a busy honeybee. Or perhaps we will discover a winding trail of ants off on some mysterious journey. They may even be marching off to do battle with the ants from a neighboring tribe. But this is not the time to follow the ants. We are anxious to see many different kinds of game today. We can return later for patient ambushes or cautious stalks.

As we approach the edge of the thicket, a little green lizard scurries

186

away into the shadows. On a sumac leaf just above his former perch sits a huge praying mantis. We will never know which one was stalking the other. In fact we would probably not even have seen the mantis if the lizard hadn't caught our attention. The proud mantis sits so quietly for hours at a time that it is necessary to examine practically every leaf of shrubs and small trees in order to find one.

The mantis is too good a specimen to pass up. She will make an especially interesting creature for your zoo if you can keep her supplied with enough living insects for food. She is not dangerous to humans, but she looks fierce enough to encourage us to flick her into a collecting jar with a twig rather than trying to pick her up with bare fingers. Of course we put her into a jar by herself, or she would eat up all our other captives.

Inside the thicket we find a little golden, fuzzy-bodied caterpillar. We have never seen one like this before, and so we are tempted to capture it. But for what purpose? Once we get it back to the zoo, we may well find that it will eat only one type of leaf and will starve to death when we are unable to decide what kind of leaf it prefers. So for now we will leave it alone, and try to identify it in some book on insects. Perhaps we will come back the next week to try to find its cocoon, then carry it home for the zoo.

The ground beneath the scrubby trees is covered with a thick, crunchy layer of dried leaves. Scraping away some of the leaves from the previous autumn, we find a spongy layer of broken leaves below this. If we dig deeper, we will find the broken leaves merging into porous, moist soil that crumbles easily in our hands.

Do you see anything in the soil that we pick up? Probably not. But now let's scoop up a double handful of the broken leaves and dark brown leafmold beneath them. We drop this mixture of crushed leaves and leafmold into a coffee can that has a coarse wire screen bottom.

coffee can sifter

We shake the can to sift the finer particles of soil out onto a square of white plastic. Look closely at the debris on the plastic and you will see spiders, earwigs, miniature beetles, and a few creatures so tiny that you can barely see them. The leafmold contains a world of its own. Many of its wonderful little creatures never see the sunlight or sniff the fresh air of the dangerous world above the surface.

We pick up our equipment now and go to explore a rotted oak log on the other side of the thicket. We don't want to destroy the log because it is home for perhaps several thousand little creatures. But we can get some idea of the wildlife inside it by carefully examining the outside and peeling away a bit of bark or a crumbling piece of wood on one end of the log. On the outside we see dozens of sawfly larvae burrows, but the larvae themselves are well inside the old log. A careful examination of the bark reveals only one or two carpenter ants, a confused old wood-boring beetle, and a crippled red wasp with ragged wings.

When we break off a piece of the rough bark, several big black beetles go scurrying right over the side of the log. In their fright they fall to the ground and plunge under the dried leaves. Scraping away the leaves where the beetles disappeared, we find a big stag beetle, a rare creature whose large head bears a pair of heavy pincers that look like the antlers of a stag. This will make an especially valuable specimen for your zoo. With a small paintbrush we scoop it up into a collecting jar.

paintbrush and jar

We could examine the old log for hours and make a large collection just from the inhabitants of its interconnecting tunnels. But we would not want to destroy it, and there is much more ahead.

Near the opposite edge of the thicket we hear a strange humming sound. We know that such a sound could mean danger, so we halt instantly and look carefully about us to see what is causing the sound.

Sure enough, about twenty feet off to our left is a large, egg-shaped, grayish paper nest of white-faced hornets. We have no intention of arguing with up to twenty thousand hornets in a tangled thicket, so we waste no time in heading off in the opposite direction.

You are able to get out into grassland on the other side much more quickly than I because of the assorted equipment that I am carrying. But because of a hornet's nest close to us, I manage to make it out rather quickly myself.

Now I have a surprise for you. There is a foot-wide, flat rock out in the field in front of us. You look at it only for a moment and see nothing. But look more closely. See that burrow on one side of it? Notice how clean this inside of it is and how fresh the loose soil around it looks. A king hornet dug that burrow just yesterday. If we waited long enough, we might see her return to it with a paralyzed cicada. If the edge were crumbling or partially covered over with debris, we would know it had been abandoned. You can never be sure what you will find if you lie in ambush near such a burrow for a while on a warm sunny day.

Now let's lift up one edge of the rock where it doesn't quite touch the ground. See the tin can sunk up to its rim in the ground beneath the rock? Inside the can are a big stag beetle and an excited searcher

tin can trap

beetle. The piece of stew meat that I used for bait is undisturbed. The beetles were attracted to the bait the night before when they left the thicket to hunt their living prey. I check the pitfall daily and change the meat every other day. When the trap is no longer being used, I will fill it in to prevent other creatures from being trapped and then starving to death. A good trapper always springs the traps that he is no longer using.

We release the stag beetle since we already have one, and they are rather rare creatures anyway. But the big green searcher beetle is a prize catch. He is picked up on a twig and shaken off into a collection jar for the zoo.

Now we go on to the marshy edge of the pond. Like the land of the leafmold, this is a world of its own. The insects are only a small part of this marshland's inhabitants, but they are all we are interested in right now. At first we cannot see anything other than an occasional minnow hiding among the cattails. Perhaps this is just not a good hunting place, so we go on farther around one side of the pond. Still nothing. I did say something about there being insects there, didn't I?

Now you will see what the third net is for. It is a peculiar-looking thing with a square net hooked onto a hickory hoe handle. The rim of the net is made of No. 12 steel wire bought at a hardware store. This doesn't really look like wire because it is almost two-tenths inch thick and was very difficult to bend. The handle is wired to one end of the square wire frame of the net. The net or bag is made of a double thickness of heavy cotton cloth.

This third net is our dip net. Dip it slowly into the water, then make a sudden drag across the bottom of the pond. Try not to pick up too much mud, or it will be too heavy to lift. It is best to sweep it through the weeds right near the pond's edge. Just one sweep, then lift it out of the water as quickly as you can. Now take a look inside. Minnows, tadpoles, a baby catfish, some squirming red worms—and two oval shaped, black diving beetles! There are a large number of other creatures almost too tiny to see, but we want those diving beetles. When you scoop them into a jar containing a little pond water, remember that they can give you a painful bite. You make several more sweeps through the water to collect some minnows, worms, fat little water fleas, and some other creatures that we do not recognize without a magnifying glass. They will go to the aquarium with the diving beetles, but only as beetle food. Few creatures will survive in the water with those little insect piranhas.

Now pull up one of the cattails and take a look at its roots. See the squirming little dragonfly nymphs crawling through the mud on the side of the roots? And do you see the little quarter-inch black flatworms with flat bodies and with heads shaped like arrow points? Cut one in half, and each half will grow into a new worm.

Let's put the dragonfly nymphs into a jar of water by themselves. If

190

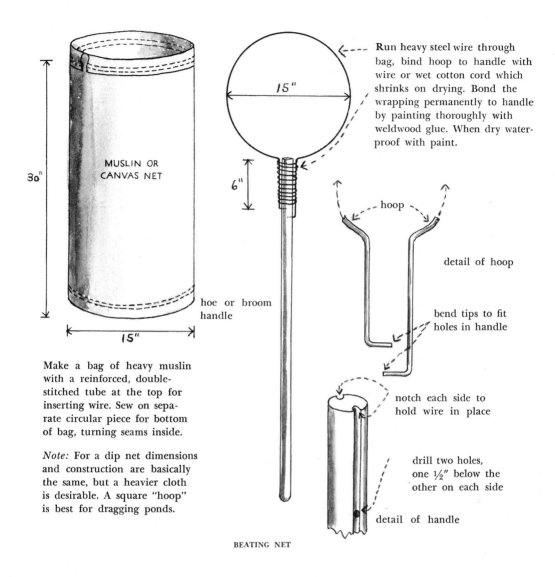

MUSLIN OR CANVAS NET

30"

15"

Make a bag of heavy muslin with a reinforced, double-stitched tube at the top for inserting wire. Sew on separate circular piece for bottom of bag, turning seams inside.

Note: For a dip net dimensions and construction are basically the same, but a heavier cloth is desirable. A square "hoop" is best for dragging ponds.

15"

6"

Run heavy steel wire through bag, bind hoop to handle with wire or wet cotton cord which shrinks on drying. Bond the wrapping permanently to handle by painting thoroughly with weldwood glue. When dry waterproof with paint.

hoop

detail of hoop

bend tips to fit holes in handle

hoe or broom handle

notch each side to hold wire in place

drill two holes, one ½" below the other on each side

detail of handle

BEATING NET

we feed them several dozen of the tiny aquatic insects, they will be quite happy in a quart fruit jar with a little pond water.

There are adult dragonflies darting back and forth along the edge of the pond, but they will be extremely hard to get even with the butterfly net. Wait until the sun goes behind a cloud, and they will settle onto weed stems and will be much easier to catch.

But we have seen enough of the wildlife of the daytime insect jungle

191

and marshland to give you an idea of what to expect. Now we return to my backyard and set up an outdoor light with a sheet under it. The light is hung about two feet above the sheet. We will be ready to try an entirely different kind of hunting as soon as it becomes dark outside. We will be lying in ambush, and the wild creatures of the jungles and marshes will be coming to us.

Almost as soon as we turn the light on, we begin to get all kinds of wild visitors. The first to come are little brown and white moths, but we are not interested in them. They are followed by an occasional golden-eyed lacewing, and then by some water beetles from the park pond. Even crickets are drawn from the surrounding grasses by the bright light. If we waited long enough, we could take a wide variety of flying specimens. But this is like driving wild horses into a hidden corral. They are nice to have if we need them, but it is more adventurous to go track them down in their own territory.

Some creatures such as luna moths can only be taken by trickery. So we must plan our hunt to take advantage of their weakness for fermented fruit juices. They may come to the light, but they are far more likely to come to a bait such as the one described in the last chapter. Tonight we go to visit some trees that I have been baiting for the past three nights. We visit them all, but there is nothing to be seen other than an occasional drab-colored little moth with a wing-spread of about 1 to 1½ inches.

If we do not have any luck at the baited trees at first, we should not give up too quickly. Sometimes the trees must be checked several times before the moths will appear. Unfortunately, this particular night we do not find a single luna moth. This sort of thing will happen sometimes in spite of our best efforts.

At least we have had an unusually good day. We managed to capture two stag beetles (we kept only one), one large searcher beetle, some crickets, a praying mantis, two diving beetles, one little white cabbage butterfly, and several dragonfly nymphs.

Tomorrow I will show you how to prepare your zoo for these wild captives. Right now it is about time to turn off the light and quit for the day.

17
The Big Game Insect Zoo

If you were trapping animals in the African forests and Asian jungles some of your captives would make tame pets with proper handling. This is also true of your insect captives. Others will remain ferocious and should be considered suitable only for exhibition in a zoo. The meat-eaters are usually the most difficult to tame, though this is not always true.

For now we must decide what to do with the wild insects we captured yesterday. Let's take the diving beetles first. You will notice that there are few if any other aquatic insects left in the jar of water with them. The meat-eating beetles are really going to be hungry today, so handle them carefully. Fortunately I have a small goldfish aquarium that was filled with water two days ago. Goldfish will live in fresh tap water, but free-living fish and insects often will not. Tap water must be allowed to stand for two or three days before it is used in an aquarium for wild creatures.

The aquarium has a thick layer of sand and pebbles on the bottom, an air pump to keep the water oxygenated for any other aquatic insects we may want to include in the aquarium, and a mass of fresh water weeds at one end. The weeds are weighted down with a small, flat rock. We do not have any soil in the aquarium, so it will probably be necessary to replace the plants in two or three weeks.

At first the beetles will probably hide in the weeds, but they will come out when you drop a few minnows or a small piece of raw, lean beef into the water. If you use the raw beef to feed them, it is best to tie a string around it so you can pull it out the next day. If you leave it in the water too long, it will spoil and ruin the water. Just remember that any changes of water must be from a bucket of water that has been allowed to stand for two or three days unless you are using pond water.

To add a more natural look to your diving beetle aquarium, you can pour in a small supply of the tiny aquatic animals that can be obtained by washing off the roots of some plants growing at the edge of a pond or lake. The mud will soon settle to the bottom of the aquarium just as it does in the pond. The diving beetles won't mind it at all.

If you plan to stock your diving beetle aquarium with a variety of living creatures such as minnows, other aquatic insects, and tadpoles, then you can take a chance on putting your dragonfly nymphs into the water also. They will probably be safe in the weeds or under a flat rock raised up on one end to make a sort of cave. A rough stick should be put into the aquarium with one end weighted down in sand or mud and the other end raised above the water. Then when the dragonfly nymphs are ready to transform into adults, they will have something on which to crawl out of the water.

There is only one thing more that you need, and that is some sort of cover over the top of the aquarium to keep the beetles from flying out at night, for they may not be too welcome in your home. The best cover is a piece of cloth stretched on a wooden frame, or a piece of wire screen cut to fit the top of the aquarium.

It was risky work getting the diving beetles transferred to their exhibition aquarium, so let's try working with something a little less dangerous. The crickets will be interesting little fellows to work with. If you are patient, you can tame them and make good pets of them. But for now let's get their cage ready.

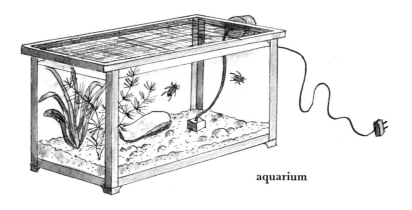

aquarium

The cricket cage may take several forms. You may want to use an aquarium with a layer of sand and rocks in the bottom, or you may prefer a box cage made of wire screen stretched across a wooden frame. Or three sides of the box could be wood with the fourth side made of a pane of clear glass or plastic. Whatever type cage you use, they will be prepared in a similar manner.

Crickets will lay their eggs readily in loose, sandy soil and seem to prefer it in their cages. They should also be provided with a hiding place made of a piece of water-soaked, rotted wood supported by small rocks about an inch or two inches high. Given such a shelter, you will

cricket cage

often find that your male crickets will climb out onto the top of the wood and chirp away as merrily as though it were night. The strange surroundings will help to subdue their fighting spirit long enough for them to get used to one another so that they probably will not get into any serious fights.

If you should have any crickets hatching out in your cage, feed them grass and clover seed for the first two days. After that they may be fed moist bread, bits of raw apple and other fruits, lettuce, moist dog biscuits, cake, and even such exotic food as fig newtons. The adults will enjoy this varied diet as much as the young ones will. If you are raising fighting crickets, they should be fed bits of raw meat and insects such as mosquitoes and fruit flies. Such a diet tends to make them aggressive. Water should never be given in a jar cap or dish. Instead, you should lightly sprinkle fresh lettuce or green grass with water when you offer it to them each day.

195

Your praying mantis will enjoy a cage similar to that prepared for the crickets, but you may want to include some living plants in a layer of slightly moistened soil. Both the plants and the mantis will enjoy several hours of sunlight a day. Of course the mantis will enjoy living any place where she can be certain that she will be well fed.

Baby mantises will thrive on a diet of fruit flies and aphids. The adults will eat houseflies, moths, caterpillars, crickets, and a variety of other insects. The little red-eyed, gnat-size fruit flies may be found around overripe bananas or other fruit in an open-air fruit stand, or you can attract them to your home by leaving a piece of overripe banana outdoors for several days.

Some mantises will eat bits of raw meat, but you may find that yours will eat only living insects that it captures for itself. If so, it should be a simple matter to capture enough small insects to keep it well fed. Like the crickets, the mantises will appreciate having their cage plants lightly sprinkled with water once a day.

You will find that the appetite of your beetles will be a combination of that of the crickets and mantises. Most beetles feed both on living flesh and on the leaves of trees and shrubs. You should offer your stag beetle various kinds of fresh tree leaves, grasses, lettuce, slices of fresh fruit, and bits of raw beef. By careful observation you will soon learn what form of food he prefers. The greater the variety of food you offer for the first week or two, the better will be your chances of keeping your captive alive and in good health. Moisture should be provided in the usual way, by sprinkling water on bits of the vegetation that you offer to your beetle.

The beetle cage may be similar to that used for the crickets. They will like a leafmold floor covering about two inches thick, a few growing plants, some old rotten sticks, and a flat rock or piece of rotted wood under which to hide during the day. A cage may be made from an aquarium, a wooden box with a glass or wire screen side for observation, or even from a large glass jar. Just remember that the beetles have wings, so it will be necessary to put a screen of some sort across the top of the cage.

Beetles are primarily night creatures, and you may not see much activity during the day. When you have any captives who come out only after dark, you may be able to fool them with colored lights. Take the cage into a darkened room and try using various colored light bulbs in a lamp. Red or yellow should give you the best results because these colors are invisible to most insects. Of course you can watch your beetles or other captives by a light of practically any color.

There are two more kinds of interesting insects that we did not capture on our hunt this time, but you will undoubtedly want to know how to care for them. We did take a little white cabbage butterfly, but we killed it for your butterfly collection. We didn't capture any ants because we didn't have time on our first hunt.

Most butterflies and moths can be kept in a large cage with several growing plants, a few twisted sticks on which to perch, and enough room to fly around the cage. The bottom may be a thick layer of sand or of slightly moistened leafmold. For food they are given a shallow container of honey diluted with water or maple syrup. The container must be covered with a wire screen to keep their feet out of it, and the liquid should come up just to the level of the screen. Butterflies and moths use a long, nectar-sucking mouth tube to drink the sweet offering. As with other insects, the plants in the cage should be lightly sprinkled with water each day.

moth and butterfly cage

Ants are very interesting insects for an observation cage. There are two ways to capture wild ants for your zoo. First of all you can build a glass-walled ant nest that is made of two foot-square panes of glass separated by two pieces of wood that are about twelve inches long and two inches thick. This gives you a sort of flat glass box open at two ends. Pack the inside with slightly moistened soil, but leave about two to three inches of space at one end which will be the top of the cage. The glass should be covered on the outside with tar paper or aluminum foil.

When the cage is ready, carefully set it over the top of a small to medium-sized ant nest. Prop it in place and leave it there for several days. If it is not in a shaded location, provide a shelter from the sun to keep it from getting too hot.

Over the next several days the confused workers in the ant colony will begin tunneling up through the soil in your observation cage. It may help to put a little honey or other bait on the top of the soil in the cage to encourage the ants to tunnel up to the open end. When you think the ants have had time to build tunnels up through the soil in your cage, slowly flood the ground around the nest with a bucket of water. As the water soaks into the ground, the nurses in the colony will rush up into the dry cage tunnels with the eggs and ant pupae. The queen will very likely go with them rather than stay and drown in her room.

About half an hour after flooding the ground, remove the cage and quickly glue or fasten a strip of wood along the open bottom. By now your cage should be filled with ants of every type in the colony. Be sure to put a wire screen or some other kind of cover over the top.

If you leave a tar paper or aluminum foil covering on the sides of the cage except when observing the ants, they will build their rooms and tunnels right up against the glass. If there is no lightproof covering on the sides, they will carefully avoid building any tunnels that are exposed to the light.

A second type of ant colony is built simply by putting one ten-inch glass baking dish inside a twelve-inch glass baking dish. The inner dish is divided into four compartments with strips of wood or plastic glued

ant colonies

into place. Each strip should have a little opening drilled or cut into it to provide for passage into the next room. One room will become a nursery, one will be the royal chamber, one will be for food storage, and the fourth will serve as a city dump for the colony.

The food room should contain a bottle cap of fresh water, bits of fatty meat or freshly killed insects, and a small container of syrup thinned with water, honey, or sugar water to provide a choice of food for the colony. Some ants will eat only meat; others will eat only sweet foods. Until you know which your colony prefers, offer them both.

To prevent the ants from escaping, the larger dish is filled with water to make a sort of moat. You should also have some sort of painted glass, wooden, or metal cover over the top of the inside dish to keep out the light. It should not fit snugly over the top of the inner dish, or the ants will be unable to get any fresh air.

The baking dish ant colony is stocked with ants taken from a colony that has been dug up and carefully spread out on a large piece of white plastic. The soil should be broken up as gently as possible to avoid injuring the queen. She may be identified by her large size and swollen abdomen. Use a wet watercolor brush for picking up individual ants such as the queen and some of the nurses and workers. They should momentarily stick to the wet brush until you can transfer them to the small baking dish. The most important thing is that you capture both the queen and as many eggs and pupae as possible. Only a few workers will be needed in such a protected colony.

If you enjoy working with your ant colony, you will probably also enjoy raising immature insects. They are often more difficult to keep alive than are the adults, but a good zookeeper can handle them. Dragonfly nymphs and young crickets are not too difficult to raise, but caterpillars and beetle larvae are quite a different kind of problem.

A caterpillar should be furnished with a variety of leaves sprinkled with water each day until you have learned which kind are preferred. Since they do little more than eat during this stage, you will not have much of a problem once you have learned the food preferences. Almost any kind of well-ventilated cage will do for a growing caterpillar. Of course they will appreciate green plants and twigs on which to climb. And when it comes time to spin the cocoon, a twig must be provided for its attachment.

Once the cocoon has been finished, the cage should be kept warm and humid. The most favorable temperature is from 70 to 85 degrees fahrenheit. A pan of water should be kept beneath the cocoon to maintain a high level of humidity around it because a butterfly will not emerge if the cocoon is kept in a dry place. As soon as the butterfly emerges, the pan can be removed. A humidity of around seventy-five percent is ideal for proper development of the pupa.

The egg case of a praying mantis will also do better in a warm, humid room. But if you put a pan of water beneath it, put a wire screen cover over it to keep the emerging young ones from drowning as they fall from the case.

200

Many insects kept in proper, large cages will breed and lay their eggs in captivity. Crickets and some aquatic insects will do this very readily, while others may never reproduce under such artificial conditions. For the best results, you must approach this problem the same as an experienced zookeeper. First learn all you can about your captives, make their cages as natural as possible, then be patient and hope for the best. When you finally do manage to raise a group of rare big game insects in captivity, it will be well worth the wait.

natural cage

18
Gateway to a Lifetime of Adventure

By this time you probably will have seen only a few of the countless adventure stories to be found in the almost completely unexplored world of the insects. You also will have learned by now that the secret to exploring this often hidden world lies in knowing where to look and what to look for. Some hunters get this information from books. Others do like the professional African hunters and get their information by observing the wildlife they seek.

One of the most famous insect hunters of all was J. Henri Fabre, a French schoolteacher who knew nothing at all about insects when he first started hunting them. Books were not of much help to him because no one else knew enough about insects to write very much about them. Fabre was so fascinated by them that he devoted his entire life to studying them in the fields and forests near his home. The knowledge that he gathered in his endless and highly adventurous search has made possible much of our own modern knowledge of the insects and their hidden world. In fact almost every book ever written about them has depended to some extent upon the observations made by Fabre in the nineteenth century.

Fabre's most interesting adventures had a way of beginning with simple acts of curiosity. For example, there was the time he brought home the cocoon of a rare European moth called the great peacock because of its beautiful purple coloration. A moth emerged from the cocoon that same day and was put in a wire screen cage for routine observation. Though Fabre could not know it at the time, this was to be the beginning of three frustrating years of tireless work.

Early that evening Fabre's young son, Paul, came running into his father's room. Paul was excited, and he kept running into the furniture, shouting all the time about the giant moths who were coming in through the kitchen windows.

Without a word, Fabre picked Paul up and ran to the kitchen with him. There they found the terrified cook bravely fighting off the invaders with her apron. She had thought at first that the giant moths were bats coming in after the insects buzzing around the kitchen lantern.

When the laughing Fabre had managed to calm his son and the cook, he explained that the moths were all males coming to see the lone female moth imprisoned in the wire cage. But when Paul asked him how the moths knew the female was there, Fabre could only give him a blank look. He would spend the next three years trying to find the answer.

At first Fabre felt certain that the males were being attracted to an odor given off by the female. He knew that some insects used their antennae to investigate odors, so he captured eight of the males and clipped off their antennae. By the next evening two of the males were dying. The other six were released outdoors.

Twenty-five males were captured that night, though only one had clipped antennae. The twenty-four new males were kept in the house all the next day; then their antennae were also clipped. Only sixteen of these were strong enough to leave the house that evening. Of the seven males captured that night, not one had clipped antennae.

Next Fabre tried marking his captives by plucking out a little patch of fur from the back of each one, leaving their antennae undisturbed. This didn't seem to make any difference. Many of the marked ones would die the next day, and those released would seldom return. Fabre couldn't understand what was happening. He kept wondering why the moths didn't come back, and why they died so quickly when the marking couldn't possibly be harming them.

By the time the female moth died nine days after her emergence, Fabre had come to the conclusion that the males lived for only a few days. During this short lifetime they did not waste time eating, mainly because not a single one of them had a mouth. It was apparent that the only purpose in life for the adult moths was to mate before dying. The males who had been released seldom returned because they were either too weak or they died soon after leaving the house.

great peacock moth (natural size)

Though he had captured a hundred and fifty moths in the space of a few nights that first spring, Fabre was unable to locate a single cocoon in a determined search in the fall of that same year. The caterpillars would spin their cocoons only on the branches of old almond trees, and there were only a few such trees in Fabre's neighborhood.

The next summer Fabre offered to pay some of the neighborhood boys for any great peacock moth caterpillars they brought to him. Eventually he was able to buy enough of these caterpillars to produce a large number of cocoons on an almond tree in his own yard. That fall he gathered the cocoons and brought them indoors for the winter.

The following spring the moths emerged at about the same time that an unseasonably cold spell turned the spring into winter for the space of a few days. The emerging moths were so weak that year that they showed little interest in any of the females who were also emerging. An occasional male moth would come in from outdoors, but they were just as disinterested as those raised by Fabre.

Still Fabre would not give up. The third year he again bought a supply of caterpillars and raised a second crop of cocoons. Nearly all the moths who emerged the following spring were healthy, so Fabre was able to resume his experiments. He was still convinced that the attraction of the males was due to some mysterious perfume given off by the female. He found that they could be locked in a poorly fitted drawer or other enclosure, and that the males would be attracted as long as the enclosure was not airtight.

Unfortunately for Fabre's theory, the moths would come flying downwind to get to the house instead of traveling against the wind as they would be expected to do in following a perfumed message. The disappointment that came with this observation was discouraging to Fabre. Though he still felt positive that the males were being attracted by an odor, he could not prove that he had the answer. Because Fabre was not the kind of man who ever took anything for granted, this was one of the few times when he was forced to admit defeat. He probably never stopped to consider that he had already learned more about the rare moths than had ever been known before.

But if Fabre was ever frustrated and discouraged by the uncooperative attitudes of the insects he studied, so the insects on his land must have been wearied and bewildered by the obstacles that he placed in their busy lives. For instance he once put a dead mouse on some loose soil beneath which he had buried a brick. Then he released half a dozen little sexton beetles next to the mouse.

The beetles immediately began burying their prize. It was only after they had lowered the body an inch or so into the ground that they discovered the brick. At this point one of the males came running out from under the mouse to have a look around. There was nothing unusual to be seen, so he returned to help the others. This went on for quite some time, with one after another of the beetles coming up for a quick look around. Finally they became so agitated at their lack of success that they began shoving the mouse first one way and then the other. Eventually they accidentally managed to roll the body over to a more desirable spot where it could be buried at last.

On another occasion Fabre tied the body of a mouse just above the ground to see if the beetles had sense enough to cut it down. When they did, he laid it on top of a coarse grass mat to see if they could cut their way through the mat. The beetles solved both problems, though Fabre was convinced that the solutions were more accidental than intelligent.

We can seldom argue with Fabre's detailed descriptions which seem to prove his points in every case. Yet Fabre would be the first to warn us that we should never assume that something is true simply because we read it in a book. He sometimes seemed to get a fiendish delight in disproving popular scientific theories about the insects he studied. He was usually right, too. Needless to say, he didn't have many more friends in the scientific world than he did in the insect world.

Experiments with the insects in their own jungles can be a risky business as two entomologists in Wisconsin once had occasion to learn. George and Elizabeth Peckham were strolling through a forest near their home when they accidently discovered a nest of yellow jackets. It was the middle of August, a time when the nest was at its maximum size.

This rare opportunity to observe the activity around a yellow jacket's

206

underground nest was too good to miss. Being naturally curious, the Peckhams were not content to sit quietly and watch the entrance of the nest. They went home and brought back several sheets of colored paper with a hole cut in the center of each one. By placing the sheets of paper over the nest one at a time they hoped to be able to determine whether or not the yellow jackets could distinguish between colors. The papers were placed with the hole over the entrance so that the yellowjackets could enter and leave the nest as usual.

When the red paper was placed around the entrance, the yellow jackets leaving the nest were not at all disturbed. But those returning to the nest were so startled that they were both confused and quite angry. Soon there were several hundred very excited yellow jackets buzzing around the heads of the Peckhams who dared not move. Finally one or two of the more adventurous yellow jackets in the group led the way back into the nest. In a few more minutes all of them were coming and going without paying any attention to the paper.

When the Peckhams dared to breathe easily again, they substituted a sheet of blue paper for the red one. The yellow jackets were apparently able to distinguish between the colors because they once again swarmed around the nest before daring to enter it. This time the Peckhams were watching from a much safer distance.

In recent years there has been at least one entomologist, Howard Ensign Evans, who was so fascinated by wasps that he started a farm on which he could raise all kinds of them. It took him quite some time to locate a nice little farm with rocky soil, large patches of brambles, broken down buildings, and a small field of sand. (His greatest difficulty was in finding a farmer who would admit that his land was really that bad.)

The farm that Professor Evans finally bought was an ideal place for wasps of practically every description. He was able to find spider-hunting wasps, bee wolves, sand wasps, caterpillar-hunting wasps, hornets, and even one peculiar little wasp who hunted stinkbugs. He found few insects that were safe from these hungry and often ferocious hunters. On the other hand there were few wasps who were safe from him.

In order to learn some of the secrets of the hunting wasps, it is necessary

207

to dig into their lairs and examine both their paralyzed prey and the young wasp larvae. This is usually easier said than done. Professor Evans dug one day into the burrow of a bee wolf that he had been observing. Since the burrow had been dug in sand, the professor thought that it would only take a little while to unearth it. He dug down about a foot, lost the winding tunnel, found it again, then lost it a second time. This went on all afternoon before he finally gave it up for the day.

The next morning he was back with a bigger shovel, determined to dig up the entire sandbank if necessary. It almost took that before he found the chambers in which the eggs had been laid on the paralyzed bees. The nest was only two or three feet back in the sandbank, but it followed a path that looked like a roller coaster track. The biggest problem was that the burrow was only a quarter of an inch thick, and the shifting sand kept caving in as he dug into it. Every time the burrow changed direction, it took quite a lot of digging to pick up the trail again. After digging in the sand for almost two days, Professor Evans was understandably pleased when he finally located the egg chambers.

Perhaps one day you will understand why someone would go to so much trouble for an insignificant-looking little killer wasp. The first time you actually spend two days in the middle of the summer digging up a hunting wasp burrow, you will understand the satisfaction of seeing something that few men have ever seen before.

Perhaps you feel by now that everything worth seeing has already been discovered. Yet no one man will ever be able to gather more than a small part of the secret knowledge of the fascinating world of the big game insects. You could spend your entire lifetime hunting and studying only insects, and you still would not be able to locate all the eight thousand different species that live within ten to twenty miles of your home. Certainly you would never be able to get a glimpse of more than a small part of the estimated eighty-two thousand different species that live in North America alone, not to mention the estimated three million species scattered throughout the world.

Now be sure to notice that I am not referring to the total number of insects, but rather to numbers of completely different types of insects. The topsoil of a single acre of fertile grassland may be the home for well over one million adult insects and insect larvae, most of which will probably be members of the same species. The total number of insects that may be found in your own state would stagger your imagination. And almost every one of them lives an unusual and often wildly adventurous life such as those that you have just read about.

If you plan to make advanced safari expeditions in future years, or if you become interested enough in the insect world to want to make a professional study of it, then you will need to go further into the details of classification so that your records will be of scientific value. Such detailed information is beyond the scope of any one book, and eventually will take you beyond all books and into the wonderful world of living biology. When you reach that point, you will be making the discoveries that others will someday be reading about.

In the meantime it will be helpful for you to know the groups to which the most common insects belong so that you can look up more information about those you are interested in hunting. Some books list insects in the index only by their scientific names, while others use only common names, and still others use both forms.

Only an occasional book will really give you all the information that you want about any one insect, and not all of these will be too accurate. But this is probably just as well. You would not enjoy hunting African big game animals if your guide told you everything there was to know about the game you were hunting. Some of the adventure of the hunt comes from learning something new about the animals you hunt and then trying to outwit them from your knowledge of their natural habits.

But whether you are an armchair hunter or an up-and-at-'em field hunter, the summary of insect orders at the back of this book should be useful to you. Genus names are shown in italic type after each common name. No species names are included because the same common name may belong to several different species that are members of the same genus. In some instances the names of several common genera are given when the common name applies to more than one genus.

The only advice that I can give you at this point is to be patient and be careful! Good luck and the best of adventures to you on your safaris.

Appendix

The Classification of Insects

With such an unbelievable number of different kinds of insects in the world, it has been necessary to develop some system for classifying them, or any worthwhile study would be impossible. First the known insects were divided into small groups in which each member of the group has certain similarities to every other member of that group, usually including the ability to mate with group members of the opposite sex to produce fertile young. These rather small groups are called *species*. The species are then grouped together with other closely related species to form a larger group called a *genus* (the plural of genus is *genera*). The members of each genus are more closely related to one another in body structure and life habits than they are to members of another genus. The genera in turn have been grouped together into different *orders,* each of which is made up of insects who appear to be more closely related to one another than they are to members of different orders. These orders are then grouped together into a single *class* known as the class Insecta. Of course every member of the class Insecta is more closely related to the other members of that class than to the members of the class Aves (birds), class Mammalia (mammals), or the class Reptilia (reptiles).

These and other classes are then grouped into a much smaller number of classifications called *phyla* (the singular of phyla is *phylum*). All of the insects, spiders, and other classes of creatures with jointed legs are members of the phylum Arthropoda. Birds, reptile, mammals, and other animals with a backbone of some sort are members of a different phylum called the Chordata. Finally we come to the last division of all, the *kingdom*. All the animals from the ameba to the elephant are classified as members of the Animal Kingdom. All plants from the single-celled algae to the giant redwood trees are classified as members of the Plant Kingdom. Deciding which kingdom a newly discovered living thing belongs in should be the easiest part of the classification procedure. Yet the amusing fact is that there exist some creatures or things that seem to fit equally well into both kingdoms.

The idea of the classification system applied to insects as well as to all

210

living things may be clearer if we consider the classification of more familiar animals such as cats and wolves. A domestic cat belongs to the species *domesticus,* a mountain lion or cougar belongs to the species *concolor,* and a timber wolf belongs to the species *lupus.* All three of these species have fur, four legs, and are almost strictly meat-eaters. Yet they do have many differences and are unable to mate with one another. Because their differences are greater than their similarities, they have been put in different species. However, the cat and the cougar still have many features in common such as retractable claws and a similar skeleton. They are much more similar to one another than they are to the wolf, so they have been put into the genus *Felis,* and the wolf has been put into the genus *Canis.* When the thousands of genera of mammals are grouped together into a broader classification by orders, both cats and the wolves go into the same order (*Carnivora,* or flesh-eaters) because they resemble one another more closely in their structure and life habits than they do the members of other orders that include such animals as cows, elephants, and giraffes. All these orders of warm-blooded mammals belong to the single class *Mammalia* which even includes human beings.

Unfortunately, none of these animals goes through life bearing a little nameplate telling how it should be classified. This business of classification is very complicated and has caused some of the most interesting arguments in the history of science. Unless you are interested in the science of classification (known as taxonomy), it might be better just to accept existing classifications and scientific names and not worry too much about how they got that way. Occasionally you will find books that give completely different names for what is apparently the same species of insect. In such a case the newest book probably gives the name that is presently being applied to that species. As more knowledge is gained about a particular species, it may be necessary to reclassify or rename it.

With a little experience it will be fairly easy for you to classify an insect belonging to one of the different orders. However, as we go farther down the family tree to genus and species, it becomes so difficult that many biologists spend their entire lives just classifying and studying the species that belong to one single genus of insects. It is customary for other biologists and naturalists to make their classification of an unknown insect as far down the family tree as the genus, then send preserved specimens to one of the usually very few scientists who specializes in that genus. If it has ever been described before, he will be able to identify it. If it proves to be a completely new species, he has the privilege of giving it a species name that may not be changed for hundreds of years.

Some of the more common insects such as the honeybees, the Amazon ant, the praying mantis, and the burying beetles may be easily recognized from their pictures in almost any well-illustrated book about insects. But for every such familiar form there will be hundreds more that may be very difficult for an amateur to classify. In general the expert's classification is based on body structure almost entirely, although the more that is known about the insect specimens, the better it will be for the classifier. On your early expeditions it will be sufficient for you to know the common names of the zoo specimens that you collect, but their scientific names have been included to help you become familiar with them.

The Insect Orders

Order Protura

The remarkable little proturans hardly look like insects. They are very primitive and still look very much as the first insects must have looked. For this reason they are of great interest to scientists. They have a very small body with a cone-shaped head that has neither eyes nor antennae. They are less than one-eighth inch long and are almost transparent, so it is no wonder that they are usually not to be found in insect collections. In fact they have only been known since 1907 when they were discovered and classified.

Both the adults and nymphs live in leafmold and in moist soil. An ideal location for finding them would be old leafmold at the edge of a forest.

Common genus of proturans: *Acerentulus*.

Order Thysanura

This is another very primitive order and is made up of three different types of insects commonly known as bristletails, silverfish, and firebrats. They are all wingless, soft-bodied little insects with long antennae and long projections extending from the tip of the abdomen or from near the tip. Their only protection is their ability to run fast and dodge even faster. Molting continues even after they become mature adults.

Eggs are laid singly in cracks, crevices, or any dark, secluded place.

The bristletails apparently live around leaves and stones outdoors. They feed on humus. The silverfish and firebrats are household pests, feeding on

212

books, clothing, or anything that contains starch. The firebrat gets its name from its preference for living quarters near furnaces or boilers where the temperature is too hot for any other insect to survive.

Common genus of bristletails: *Mesomachilis.*

Common genus of silverfish: *Lepisma.*

Common genus of firebrats: *Thermobia.*

Order Collembola

The springtails are very small wingless insects with antennae and legs which are well developed. They rather resemble tiny fleas except that they use their springlike "tail" for hopping instead of using their legs as fleas do. The jumping organ is an extension of the abdomen that is usually hooked on the underside of the body. When it is released, the springing action flips the insect into the air. A few species do not have this jumping organ.

The springtails are most often found in moist places such as leafmold, rotted logs, at the edges of ponds and streams, and in damp soil.

Little is known about the egg laying of the springtails. A few species lay their eggs singly or in clusters in humus or damp soil.

Common genera of springtails: *Isotoma, Achorutes,* and *Neosminthurus.*

Order Ephemeroptera

The adults of this order are commonly called mayflies or shad flies. They are slender insects with soft bodies and two pairs of net-veined wings. The hind pair of wings is much smaller than the front pair. The hairlike antennae are so tiny that they appear to be missing unless the insect is seen at very close range. Two or three hairlike projections extend out from the tip of the abdomen. These are sometimes longer than the rest of the body.

The young, known as mayfly nymphs, may live for several years in the waters of a pond or lake. They feed on plants and animals smaller than themselves. When they emerge from the water, they crawl up on a rock or plant stem and molt into a winged but still immature form. A day or two later another molt will produce the mature adult. At times the mayflies will emerge in such vast numbers that they form dancing clouds above the surface of lakes and streams.

The adults usually live only long enough to mate and lay their eggs before dying. Their eggs may require a few weeks or a month to hatch. Other species may live for several weeks, carrying their fertilized eggs about inside

213

their bodies until the young are nearly ready to hatch. When they finally do lay their eggs, the young hatch out almost as quickly as the egg hits the water.

Common genera of mayflies: *Hexagenia, Ephemera, Callibaetis,* and *Cloeon.*

Order Odonata

The dragonflies and damselflies may be slender or have stout bodies. Their two pairs of net-veined wings are quite similar and are both about the same size. Their antennae are very tiny and hairlike. The abdomen may be very long but does not have any tail-like projections.

The young are called nymphs. They are aquatic but do not swim. Instead they walk around on the muddy bottom of a pond or lake looking for prey small enough to capture. Some will wait in ambush behind a small stone or on the side of a water plant. Nymphs of some smaller species may mature in one year. Others take up to four years before becoming adults. When full grown the nymph will climb out of the water and attach itself to a stick or weed stem for the final molt. The newly emerged adult may require one or two days of resting before it becomes hard enough for hunting.

The adults have the strange habit of flying along head-to-tail during the mating period. When it comes time to lay the eggs, the male almost always helps the female while she lays the eggs in or under the water. At times he will swoop down and pull her out of the water when she comes to the surface after laying an egg on the muddy bottom. At other times he provides a fighter escort, driving other males out of his territory while the female lays her eggs.

Common genera of dragonflies: *Macromia, Libellula,* and *Anax.*

Common genera of damselflies: *Lestes, Enallagma,* and *Hetaerina.*

Order Dictyoptera

This order includes several different groups of easily recognizable insects. The first group is made up of the praying mantises, including two imported species which are known as the European mantis and the Oriental mantis. These insects are medium size to large, and can measure as much as four inches long when fully grown. The thorax is long and slender. The front legs are very muscular and bear many sharp spines on their underside. The middle and hind legs are slender and are about the same length.

All mantises are meat-eaters. In fact they may even eat one another. In

214

some species the female usually kills and eats the male either during or just after mating. Few creatures in the insect jungles are more feared than these monsters. But in spite of their fearsome appearance, they are quite harmless.

The second group is made up of the cockroaches. They are flat insects which are able to run rapidly. They have long, slender antennae and a pair of short, stiff projections that extend from the tip of the abdomen. These projections, known as cerci, may be covered by the wings of some species. Other species have no wings at all. When wings are present, the front pair is nothing more than a leathery covering for the more fragile, membranous hind wings that fold up when not in use.

The cockroaches are typically tropical insects, but some of the more hardy species may be found in the north living under bark of trees or in rotten logs. The German cockroach and the Oriental cockroach are among the biggest household pests in North America, but they are not native to this country. Most of the native species prefer to live outdoors.

As you probably know, the cockroaches will eat just about anything that they can chew up and swallow. This must be to their advantage, for they have remained almost unchanged for about three hundred million years.

The third group will be easy to recognize if you can find them. These are the walking sticks, green or brown insects who have such long and slender bodies that they look almost exactly like a dried twig. The smaller species are only half an inch long, while some may be as much as six inches long.

They are strict vegetarians. Their food consists of tree leaves and of the soft parts of some plants, particularly the subtropical plants often found in the southern states.

Common genera of mantids: *Mantis, Paratenodera,* and *Stagmomantis.*

Common genera of cockroaches: *Cryptocercus, Blattella, Blatta,* and *Periplaneta.*

Common genera of walking sticks: *Diapheromera* and *Megaphasma.*

Order Orthoptera

The members of this order should also be easy to recognize. These are the jumping insects including the grasshoppers, crickets, katydids, mole crickets, and pygmy locusts. They are medium size to large, characteristically having long hind legs with muscular thighs for leaping. The large head bears a pair of long antennae and well-developed eyes. The thorax is covered with a bony plate that looks rather like a large, stiff collar.

215

The members of this order are all vegetarians, but they will eat meat on occasion if they get hungry enough.

Eggs are usually deposited in the soil, though the tree crickets prefer to lay theirs in a hole drilled into the stem of a soft-bodied shrub. The young of all species in this order resemble their parents at all stages of development from the time they hatch out of the egg.

Common genera of grasshoppers: *Schistocerca, Melanoplus, Acrydium, Conocephalus,* and *Camnula.*

Common genera of crickets: *Ceuthophilus, Nemobius, Oecanthus, Gryllotalpa,* and *Tridactylus.*

Common genera of katydids: *Microcentrum* and *Amblycorypha.*

Order Grylloblattodea

The single representative of this order is an interesting little creature called a grylloblattid because it has no other common name. It has an elongate, slender body made of many segments, slender legs, and no wings at all. Interestingly enough these creatures are found only in places that are covered with snow for the greatest part of the year. They live in leafmold, rotten logs, and under stones, coming out only to feed on vegetation and decaying organic materials.

The female lays her little black eggs in humus or damp moss.

The only genus of grylloblattids: *Grylloblatta.*

Order Isoptera

The members of this order are the termites, sometimes called white ants. These insects are medium size, with soft, white bodies. They live in colonies similar to those of ants, but there the resemblance ends. The termites are not even as closely related to the ants as are the bees and wasps.

The typical termite colony has three different social levels: workers, soldiers, and reproductives (kings and queens). In the spring and fall a large number of winged kings and queens are produced within the colony. These soon swarm out of the main entrance, spread out over the surrounding countryside, mate, and then begin new colonies if suitable places can be found before they die of exhaustion or starvation.

The workers are responsible for feeding the entire colony; yet none of the termites is able to digest dried wood which forms the main part of their diet. Fortunately for them their stomachs contain microscopic animals

216

called protozoa, These millions of protozoa digest the wood for them, turning it into materials that the termite's body is able to use as food.

Common genus of termites: *Reticulitermes*.

Order Plecoptera

These are the stone flies, medium-sized to large insects often found clinging to damp rocks or to the trunks of trees near ponds and streams. They have long antennae and a pair of projections ranging in size from short to long extending from the tip of the abdomen. These cerci are similar to those of the cockroaches, though usually much longer. Both pairs of transparent wings are veined and are about the same size, although the front pair is usually more narrow than the hind pair. Adults may live for several weeks.

The nymphs of all stone flies are aquatic. They live under stones, in the cracks of submerged logs, and in piles of debris that gather near the shore. Most of them are vegetarians, though a few of them feed on small insects or other aquatic creatures small enough for them to capture.

The adult females lay hundreds to thousands of eggs, simply dropping them into the water without a backward glance. The eggs soon hatch, but the young may live in the water for a year or two before crawling out onto a rock or weed stem to prepare for the final molt. The wings harden enough for flight within a few minutes of the completion of the molt.

Some species which emerge from the water in fall or winter seem to prefer crawling over concrete bridges. They may often be collected in great numbers from such a location in the cool months of the year.

Common genera of stone flies: *Allocapnia, Isoperla, Pteronarcys,* and *Neophasganophora*.

Order Dermaptera

This is the order of earwigs, insects ranging from small to medium size and characterized by a pair of strong pincers which protrude from the tip of the abdomen. When wings are present, the front pair is nothing more than a hard covering for the protection of the more delicate, fan-shaped pair of hind wings. The antennae are long and slender.

The earwig's common name comes from an ancient belief that they would crawl into the ear of a sleeping person and then refuse to come out. It is true that they are most active at night, but they prefer hiding in leaf-mold and under rocks to hiding in the ear of any kind of animal.

217

They are scavengers who eat a variety of foods. A few species are carnivorous, and at least one is destructive to roses, dahlias, and other flowers.

The earwigs are among the very few insects that have any kind of home life in which the parents take care of their young. When the eggs are laid, the female stands guard over them. Even after the young ones have hatched, she will remain with them for a short time.

Common genera of earwigs: *Labia* and *Forficula*.

Order Embioptera

The members of this rather uncommon order live primarily in tropical areas, though a few species are found in the southern United States. They are known as embiids or web spinners. The body is long and the legs short. The front feet are enlarged because they are used in spinning the silken web in which the embiid lives. Their silken tunnels may be found on the ground, under loose bark on an old log, or among lichens growing on a tree stump. They will often build silken nets under matted leaves or under dry stones. They tend to live in large colonies of interconnecting tunnels.

Most species have both males and females, but a few have females only. Like the earwigs, the female embiid stays near her cluster of eggs and watches over her young after they hatch.

Common genus of embiids: *Oligotoma*.

Order Psocoptera

Some species of the fat-bodied but tiny psocids are commonly called booklice. They have jaws for chewing their food, though this food consists mostly of soft or decaying vegetable matter. They prefer to live outdoors, but may come indoors at times if the inside of the house is damp. Outdoors they may be found in a wide variety of locations such as clumps of dried grass, leafmold, on the bark of trees, on shaded rocks, in birds' nests, and under fence posts. Those outdoors are called barklice.

A few species are slow in their movements, but most of them are able to move with surprising speed. They have been referred to as some of the most rapid dodgers of all of the insects.

When the female lays her eggs on the surface of a leaf or on a bit of tree bark, she spins a cover of silken threads to anchor them in place. From one to ten eggs are usually deposited in a single location.

Common genera of psocids: *Liposcelis* and *Trogium*.

218

Order Zoraptera

The zorapterans are among the rarest insects known. There are only sixteen species in the entire order, two of which are found in the southeastern United States. They look somewhat like tiny termites except that their legs are longer in relation to the size of their bodies, and the body is covered with stiff bristles so tiny that they can be seen only under a very powerful magnifying glass. The body of the much longer termite is smooth.

Colonies of a few to as many as a hundred zorapterans may be found in rotten wood or under the bark of old logs or stumps. They are believed to be scavengers. There is no evidence that the members of the colony work together as do the social insects such as ants and bees.

Eggs are apparently laid in the runways of the colony and then left to themselves. The young hatch out in about three weeks.

Only genus in the world to date: *Zorotypus*. (Two species in North America, both of which live in the southern states.)

Order Mallophaga

These tiny wingless creatures are external on birds and on a few mammals. Because of their preference for birds they are often called bird lice. And because of their greedy habit of chewing up fur, feathers, and skin of the animals they infest, they are also known as chewing lice. Each species has a different type of host. None of these parasitizes man.

The adult chewing lice vary a great deal in shape and habits. They may be long and slender, short and fat, covered with fine hair or almost bald. Some are very fast on their feet; others are very slow. The eggs, which are glued to the hair or feathers of the host, also come in a variety of types. Some of the species lay very plain eggs, while others lay eggs decorated with barbs or with tufts of hair.

Common genera of chewing lice: *Columbicola* and *Menacanthus*.

Order Anoplura

These are the bloodsucking lice who are spread among humans living in crowded, unsanitary places. They cannot fly, but must depend upon being so close to their prospective victims that they can climb off one and onto the other. Because they are able to carry dangerous microbes, they are able to spread some human diseases such as typhus or "jail fever."

The adults are tiny, wingless insects with flat bodies and look somewhat

219

like a little crab when seen under a powerful magnifying glass. Various species infest such animals as horses, sheep, dogs, cattle, wild rodents, and pigs. The eggs are glued to the hair of the host.

Common genera of sucking lice: *Pediculus* and *Haematopinus*.

Order Thysanoptera

These tiny pests, known as thrips, spread plant diseases as they travel from one plant to another. They have sucking mouthparts for drinking the sap of soft plants that they feed upon. They are unable to do much damage themselves, but the microbes they carry will spread to many plants growing in the area. A few species kill and eat other tiny insects such as mites.

The thrips are found most commonly in flowers. They may be found in almost any blossom if it is broken open very carefully and examined around the base of the center of the flower.

A few species of thrips have fringes of long hair on their wings which makes them quite unlike the wings of any other insect.

The eggs of thrips are laid on the surface of plants in some protected spot.

Common genera of thrips: *Anaphothrips, Heterothrips,* and *Heliothrips.*

Order Hemiptera

There are fifty-five thousand or more species in this order alone. They include some of the worst pests known to man. Among these are the bedbugs, aphids, and scale insects. Less destructive species include the cicada, leafhopper, treehopper, spittlebug, and many others. The order is divided up into two groups, each of which is sometimes considered to be a separate order rather than members of the same order.

One of the two groups is made up of the "true" bugs. Although insects in general are sometimes called bugs by people who know little about them, only members of this group actually are true bugs. A pointed beak on the front of the head is kept tucked under the body when it is not being used to drink the sap of plants or the blood of insects or other animals. When wings are present, the base of the front wings is rather leathery, becoming more membranous near the tip. The hind wings are entirely membranous. The adults come in a great variety of shapes and sizes, ranging from a fraction of an inch to several inches in length.

The eggs are laid either singly or in groups that are glued to the stems or leaves of plants. Some species insert their eggs into the plant tissue.

220

The nymphs of most true bugs closely resemble the adult forms.

The second group of this order is made up entirely of vegetarians. When wings are present, the front wings may be either leathery or membranous but not both at the same time. The back wings are always membranous. Many species do not have any wings at all.

Common genera of true bugs: *Murgantia* (harlequin bug), *Anasa* (squash bug), *Blissus* (chinch bug), *Phymata* (ambush bug), *Pselliopus* (assassin bug), *Cimex* (bedbug), *Gerris* (water strider), *Notonecta* (backswimmer), *Arctocorixa* (water boatman), and *Atheas* (lace bug).

Common genera of the second group: *Ceresa* (treehopper), *Magicicada* (cicada or seventeen-year locust), *Draeculacephala* (leafhopper), *Aphis* (aphid), *Aspidiotus* (scale insect), *Aphrophora* (spittlebug), and *Pseudo-coccus* (mealybug).

Order Neuroptera

This order consists of the lacewing flies whose larvae are called aphis lions, fish flies, alderflies, dobsonflies, and ant lions. The adults are very small to large insects usually having two pairs of transparent wings crisscrossed with a great number of fine veins that give them the appearance of a net.

Both the adults and the larvae are carnivorous. The adults will likely be seen less often than their ferocious larvae because the adults are usually most active at dusk or at night.

The young of most of the species spin silken cocoons with the aid of silk glands located in little tubes in the abdomen.

Common genera of neuropterans: *Corydalus* (dobsonfly), *Chrysopa* (golden-eye lacewing whose larvae are called aphis lions), *Myrmeleon* (ant lion), and *Sialis* (alderfly).

Order Coleoptera

With over 227,000 species this is the largest of all the animal orders in the world. Almost 30,000 different species live in North America from the land of eternal frost in northern Canada to the dry desert country along the Mexican border. Beetles may be easily told from other orders of insects by means of the leathery front wings that lie flat along the back and meet in a straight line right down the middle. The hind wings are usually folded beneath the protective armor of the front wings. A very few of the more rare species do not have wings at all.

Some beetles are so tiny that they can safely live in the middle of a colony of hungry red ants. They are not only too tiny to make even one mouthful for an ant, they are also too fast to make it worthwhile for the ant to chase them. Other beetles that live in tropical countries such as the jungles of New Guinea are so large that tiny forests of moss and lichens are sometimes found growing on the beetles' backs.

Beetles have chewing mouthparts and a wide variety of tastes in food. They will eat almost anything that was once alive, and many of them will not hesitate to attack and eat other insects. The appetites of some species such as the Japanese beetle make them serious pests, while the appetites of others such as the aphid-destroying ladybug make them very valuable friends of man.

The beetles are among the very few insects whose larvae bear common names unlike those of the adult. The grubworm, larva of the June bug or May beetle, is prized by cane pole fishermen as a bait for perch. These same fishermen may find larvae of other beetles apparently taking revenge for the killing of their cousins by cutting down young tomato plants in the fisherman's vegetable garden. These are the wireworms, larvae of the snapping or click beetles.

The eggs of beetles are oval or round and are laid in spring or early summer and hatch out one or two weeks later. The larvae usually grow to full size during the summer, then pupate in the soil. The adults emerge within a few weeks and have completely matured by winter. They hibernate during the cold months, then come out and lay their eggs a short time before they will die.

Common genera of beetles: *Lucanus* (stag beetle), *Copris* (dung beetle), *Harpalus* (ground beetle), *Phyllophaga* (May beetle), *Photinus* (firefly), *Melanotus* (click beetle or wireworm), *Anthrenus* (carpet beetle), *Coccinella* (ladybug), *Epicauta* (blister beetle), *Popillia* (Japanese beetle), *Dynastes* (rhinoceros beetle), *Anthonomus* (boll weevil), *Cicindela* (tiger beetle), *Dytiscus* (predacious diving beetle), *Dineutes* (whirligig beetle), and many, many others.

Order Strepsiptera

This is the rare order of twisted wing flies, a rather good description of the males whose wings are shaped like bent fan blades. All the females in the order, whether parasitic or not, are wingless. Most species are parasitic

222

on other insects. Some of the adult females are nothing more than tiny egg factories living in or on the body of the host insect. They have no antennae, eyes, or legs. The adult female never leaves her original host.

Genus of twisted wing flies: *Stylops.*

Order Mecoptera

The scorpion fly males look like flying scorpions though the "stings" are actually harmless. The female does not even have the fake sting. One group of the scorpion flies doesn't fly because its members do not have wings.

The adults live mainly on insects that they capture, though they will occasionally eat nectar, fruits, and mosses. One group captures other insects for food by using its hind legs as a trap while hanging from a twig with its front legs. That is a pretty good trick.

The oval-shaped eggs are laid in the ground, either singly or in clusters of a hundred or more. The larvae may be found in moss, rotten wood, or in mud and humus near a woodland pond or stream. They spend the pupal stage in the ground.

Common genus of scorpion fly: *Panorpa.*

Order Trichoptera

These are the caddis flies. Their larvae, naturally enough, are called caddisworms. Adults of the various species range in length from about one-sixteenth inch to almost two inches. They almost all look like small, hairy moths except that they have chewing mouthparts instead of the sucking mouthparts of the moths.

The caddis fly females lay from several hundred to a thousand eggs each. The females of some species enter the water and lay masses of eggs on stones or other objects. Others will deposit their eggs on tree branches overhanging the water in which the larvae and pupae will live. The larvae live in both lakes and streams, preferring cold water.

The caddisworms look like caterpillars, often live in portable houses, and sometimes spin silken nets in running water to catch the bits of plant and animal matter upon which they feed. Their chief food supply consists of tiny plants and animals including the larvae of other insects.

When the caddisworm is ready to pupate, it spins a cocoon of silk which may include bits of sand and debris picked up by accident. After two to three weeks the pupa chews its way out of the cocoon, swims to the surface, and climbs out of the water where it completes the change into an adult.

Common genera of caddis flies: *Ptilostomis, Rhyacophila, and Limnophilus.*

Order Lepidoptera

The young of these creatures look like prehistoric monsters, eat almost constantly, and will eat just about anything of plant origin. Only a very few species have carnivorous larvae.

The adult moths and butterflies have two pairs of large wings. They have a coiled tongue that looks rather like a watch spring when they are not using it to drink the nectar from flowers. A few species are not really particular about what they eat and would just as soon feed on the juices of a dead animal as on the sweetest blossom. A very few adults live such a short time that they do not have any mouthparts at all. They are too busy mating and laying eggs to bother with eating anyway.

In your lifetime you have probably seen only a very few of the more than ten thousand species of these insects which live in the United States. These are the moths and butterflies!

You have probably thought that the wings of the moths and butterflies were covered with a fine, colored powder. Actually, this is not powder at all. Rather it consists of a horny substance in the shape of a scale. The light reflected from thousands of these different scales gives the wings their brilliant colors.

Common genera of moths: *Tinea* (clothes moth), *Thyridopteryx* (bagworm), *Sanninoidea* (peach tree borer), *Loxostege* (webworm), *Malacosoma* (tent caterpillar), *Callosamia* (promethea moth), *Carpocapsa* (codling moth), *Samia* (cecropia moth), and *Alsophila* (cankerworm).

Common genera of butterflies: *Proteides* (skipper), *Iphiclides* (zebra swallowtail), *Pieris* (cabbageworm), *Minois* (grayling), *Lycaena* (American copper), *Colias* (orange sulfur), *Lycaenopsis* (spring azure), *Vanessa* (red admiral), and *Polygonia* (question mark).

Order Diptera

Many insects bear the name of "fly" just as many insects are often referred to as "bugs." However, this is the only order of true flies. Almost twenty thousand species of these live in North America. They have four wings; yet they are called two-winged flies because the hind pair is mere stubs

224

used as stabilizers. Only the well-developed front pair of wings is used for flying. These hungry creatures will eat anything from flower nectar to human blood, as long as the food is liquid. The mosquitoes and some of the biting flies in this order are able to spread serious diseases.

Fly larvae, most of which are called maggots, are very unusual little creatures even for a world which is full of novelties. Their heads are usually so tiny that they can be pulled back into the body. They seldom have legs. They must live in moist places since they have no protective covering such as most insect larvae have. These living quarters may be anything from a pond or a mud puddle to the inside of a living animal, depending upon the species of fly. And perhaps just to be different the larvae do not spin cocoons at all. In fact the individuals of some species turn into pupae inside the skin they occupied when they were larvae.

The eggs of most species are simple, oval or elongated, and are normally laid individually either in, on, or near the food on which the larvae will live. In a few species the eggs hatch just before they leave the body of the female. And in one species known as the sheep ticks, the larvae hatch and grow to full size while they are still inside the female!

Common genera of flies: *Epiphragma* (cranefly), *Aedes* (mosquito), *Simulium* (blackfly), *Musca* (housefly), *Aphidoletes* (midge), *Tabanus* (horsefly), *Didea* (flowerfly) *Drosophila* (fruit fly), *Gasterophilus* (botfly), *Hypoderma* (warble fly), *Melophagus* (sheep tick), *Culicoides* (sand fly), and *Calliphora* (bluebottle fly).

Order Siphonaptera

These are the fleas, parasites of all warm-blooded animals. They are small, tough, and elusive. Their flattened bodies are designed to make it a simple matter for them to slip rapidly through the hair of even the thickest-furred animal. They have no wings, but this doesn't bother the hardy flea. His hind legs enable him to jump an enormous distance as compared to his tiny size.

When fleas occupy household pets, they may often be found about the house because they are great travelers. As soon as they have made a meal on one host, they are likely to hop off and go exploring for different food. Fleas carried by the millions of rats in medieval Europe were responsible for the black plague that almost wiped out the entire human population of the continent. The fleas carried the germs from the rats to humans.

The larvae of fleas have a less dainty appetite than their parents. Their

225

most usual source of food is the droppings of the adults. Like most insects, the flea larvae spin silken cocoons when the time comes for them to be changed into the resting pupal stage.

Common genera of fleas: *Ctenocephalides* (dog and cat fleas), *Echidnophaga* (sticktight flea), and *Xenopsylla* (rat flea, sometimes the carriers of bubonic plague germs).

Order Hymenoptera

This order is made up of more than fifteen thousand different species of ants, bees, wasps, hornets, sawflies, ichneumon flies, horntails, and many other less commonly known but equally interesting insects.

When wings are present, the front pair is usually so much larger than the back pair that they may often appear to be two-winged insects. The membranous front and hind wings have tiny hooks at the edges where they meet. These hooks serve to hold the wings together when the insect is flying. The mouthparts are designed for chewing, but many of the species have mouths that are adapted for sucking as well since the diet of the members of this order is usually a liquid.

This order is divided into a thick-waisted group made up of sawflies and horntails, and a narrow-waisted group which includes wasps, bees, and ants.

The larvae of the sawflies and horntails look somewhat like caterpillars. Almost all of them are plant-eaters.

The larvae of the group with narrow waists look more like maggots or legless beetle larvae. Some of them are able to get their own food, but most of them live in nurseries where busy nurses bring food to them.

The members of this order are the most useful to man of all of the insects. They are the honey-makers, the insect pest destroyers, and the pollinators who make possible the growth of many important plants. The social groups of this order also have the distinction of having learned to live together in communities in which almost every individual is a hard worker and an unselfish part of the whole.

Common genera of sawflies and horntails: *Cimbex* (sawfly), *Neodiprion* (sawfly), *Tremex* (horntail wasp), and *Nematus* (imported currant worm).

Common genera of wasps, bees, and ants: *Glypta* (ichneumon fly), *Vespa* (bald-faced hornet), *Monomorium* (little black ant), *Apis* (honeybee), *Pheidole* (harvest ant), *Formica* (gray ant), *Amphibolips* (gall wasp), *Pepsis* (tarantula hawk), and *Megachile* (leafcutting bee).

226

Glossary

Abdomen: the tail end of the insect; the third and last major segment of the insect body.

Antennae: the feelers; flexible, threadlike or sometimes bushy projections on the front of the head of many insects. These may be the means by which the insects hear and smell. Apparently they serve insects in finding their way about and in communicating with others of their kind.

Anterior: the front or head end of the body.

Apiary: a place where bees are kept.

Appendage: a part of the insect that sticks out from the body, such as a leg or antenna.

Basal: relating to the base of an appendage; that part of an appendage that is attached to the body.

Brood: the young of insects, usually referring to many larvae living in the same colony; the similar term "foul brood" refers to a bacterial disease of honeybee larvae.

Carnivorous: meat eating; the type of insect that kills and eats other insects or small animals.

Carrion: decaying flesh.

Cephalothorax: the combined head and chest of an insect.

Cerci: a pair of simple or segmented appendages situated at the posterior end of the abdomen of some insects such as mayflies and cockroaches.

Chemoreceptors: sense organs such as the antennae; these organs are used for tasting and smelling.

Chitin: a tough, flexible layer of material that lies between the outer shell and the soft skin of an insect.

Chrysalis: the pupa or cocoon of moths and butterflies.

Cocoon: the silken envelope which an insect larva spins about itself when it is ready to pupate.

Colony: a group of the same species of insects living together.

Compound eye: an eye that is made up of many separate lenses.

Coxa: the short, jointed part of the insect leg that is attached to the thorax.

Crop: a muscular storage pouch located midway between the insect's mouth and stomach. Food swallowed by the insect is stored in the crop before passing on to the stomach for complete digestion. Some insects will regurgitate, or cast back up, food from the crop and use it to feed other insects in their colony, or they may use it to feed their young.

Cuticle: the outer layer of the insect's body; the nonliving part of the armor.

Distal: that part of an appendage that is farthest from the body; opposite of proximal.

Dorsal: the area of the back; the upper side.

Elytra: the wing covers of a beetle.

Embryo: a young insect still within the egg; an unborn, living creature.

Endoskeleton: an internal skeleton such as that of mammals.

Entomologist: a biologist who specializes in the study of insects.

Entomology: the branch of science that deals with insects.

Epicuticle: the usually waxy outer layer of the cuticle.

Epidermis: the thin layer of skin cells that produce the material of which the cuticle is formed; the outer layer of the living skin.

Exoskeleton: an external skeleton; one that covers the outside of an animal such as an insect.

External: outside the body.

Femur: the upper part of the leg joined to the short coxa.

Fertilization: the process in reproduction which unites the male and female cells so that a new individual of the species can be developed.

Filiform: threadlike.

Gall: an abnormal growth on a leaf or plant stem, often caused by an insect larva developing in the plant tissue.

Genus: a group of closely related species of animals.

Grub: a beetle larva; also, the larvae of some flies.

Honeydew: a sweet fluid excreted by certain insects such as the aphids; sometimes called ant food because of the great love that ants have for it.

Host: an insect or animal which provides food and sometimes shelter for another insect, called its parasite.

Instar: the period of time between two successive molts of an insect.

Internal: inside the body.

Labium: the lower lip of an insect.

Labrum: the upper lip of an insect.

Larva: a grubworm; a wormlike stage in the development of an insect that undergoes a complete metamorphosis.

Mandibles: the insect jaws; the pincers or "pinchers" of an insect.

228

Metabolism: the chemical changes taking place in the living body.

Metamorphosis: the series of changes from the immature stage to the adult stage of an insect; most commonly this process is a complete metamorphosis in which the young have no resemblance to the adult. Moths and butterflies, which first appear as caterpillars, are examples of this process of complete change. Incomplete metamorphosis refers to the growth of those insects in which the young are small models of the adult from the time they are hatched. Grasshoppers furnish an example of incomplete metamorphosis.

Molting: the replacement of an old skin by a new one.

Nectar: the sweet fluid found in the blossoms of many flowers; a natural mixture of sugars and water.

Nymph: the immature stage of an insect that undergoes an incomplete metamorphosis (see "metamorphosis").

Ocelli: single lens eyes found on the insect's head between the much larger compound eyes.

Omnivorous: the type of insect that eats both vegetation and animal flesh.

Ovipositor: the egg-laying tool of a female insect.

Palps: fleshy, fingerlike projections on the jaws of insects.

Parasite: a living organism that obtains its food and sometimes its shelter from another organism.

Plankton: aquatic, mostly microscopic plants and animals.

Predacious: predatory; describes an animal that hunts other animals for food.

Protein: the complex molecules that form the greatest part of the muscles of animals; protein may also be combined with other materials to form a substance such as chitin.

Proximal: opposite of distal; that part of an appendage closest to the body.

Pupa: that stage in the metamorphosis of an insect in which the insect rests inactive in a cocoon; the stage in which an insect has stopped eating and is transforming into its adult structure.

Queen: the female insect capable of laying fertile eggs; usually refers to an egg-laying female insect who produces all of the fertile eggs for a colony of insects.

Regurgitate: to cast back up from the crop (or stomach) partially digested food which is often fed to the young.

Royal jelly: a secretion from special head glands of young honeybees.

Scale: a modified hair with a broad and flattened shape.

Sclerotin: a horny material containing protein. It forms the outer shell of an insect.

Species: a class or group of insects, similar in appearance, having the same physical characteristics, and called by the same name.

Spiracle: an air vent; an opening into the breathing tubes of an insect.

Swarm: a large-scale migration of insects of the same species; a queen and a group of her followers who have left an old colony to begin a new one.

Tarsus: the segments that make up the foot of an insect.

Taxonomy: the science of animal and plant classification.

Thorax: the middle section of an insect; the part of the body between the head and abdomen.

Tibia: the part of an insect's leg that is joined to the femur at its upper end and to the tarsus at the lower end; the lower leg.

Trachea: an air tube that carries air from the spiracle to the tissues of an insect (insects do not have lungs).

Vegetarian: the type of insect that eats only vegetation.

Ventral: the underside; opposite of dorsal.

Voracious: greedy, an eager eater.

Index

The scientific names for the genera of the insects mentioned in this book are in *italics*. All orders, classes, and phyla are in SMALL CAPS. A number in **boldface** indicates an illustration.

Butterflies
  care of, 186, 197
  classification and description, 224
  see also individual names of
      monarch butterfly
      red admiral butterfly
Butterfly trees, **178, 179**

Cabbageworm, 224
Caddis flies, 223-24
Caddisworms, 223
Calliphora, 225
Callibaetis, 214
Callosamia, 224
Calosoma (searcher beetle), 87
Camnula, 216
Camponotus (carpenter ant), 135
Cankerworm, **130,** 224
Canis, 211
Carnivora, 211
Carolina mantis, 23, **23**
  see also mantises
Carpet beetle, 222
Carpenter ants, 51, 132-36, **134, 136**
  classification and description, 135-
      36
  hunting guide, 135-36
  names for, 135
Carpocapsa, 224
Cat, 211
Caterpillar hunter, 135
Caterpillars
  care of, 200
  tent, **12**
Cecropia moth, 224
Ceuthophilus, 216
Ceresa, 221
Chinch bug, 221
CHORDATA, 210

Chrysopa (lacewings), 99, 221
Cicada killer wasp, 102-7, **104,** 111-
      13, **111**
  care of, 105-7
  classification and description, 111
  hunting guide, 111-13
Cicada
  classification and description,
      220-21
  enemies, *see* cicada killer wasp
Cicindela, 222
Cimbex, 226
Cimex, 221
Classification, insect, 210-26
Click beetle, 222
Cloeon, 213-14
Clothes moth, 224
Coccinella (ladybug), 99, 222
Cockroaches, 215
Codling moth, 224
COLEOPTERA, 221-22
Colias, 224
Collecting tools, *see* equipment
COLLEMBOLA, 213
Columbicola, 219
Concolor, 211
Conocephalus, 216
Copris, 222
Corydalus, 221
Cougar, 211
Cranefly, 225
Crickets, 12, **78-79,** 119-24, **122**
  care of, 194-95, 201
  classification and description, 123-
      24, 215-16
  hunting guide, 123-24
  names for, 123
Cross-pollination, 170
Cryptocercus, 215

Bibliography

Barker, Will. *Familiar Insects of America.* New York: Harper & Row, 1960.

Brues, Charles T. *Insect Dietary: An Account of the Food Habits of Insects.* Cambridge: Harvard University Press, 1946.

Chu, Hung-fu. *How to Know the Immature Insects.* Dubuque, Iowa: William C. Brown Company, Publishers, 1949.

Comstock, J. H. *An Introduction to Entomology.* 9th ed. rev. Ithaca, N.Y.: Comstock Publishing Associates, 1940.

Crompton, John. *The Hunting Wasp.* Boston: Houghton Mifflin Company, 1955.

Evans, Howard E. *Wasp Farm.* Garden City, N.Y.: Doubleday & Company, 1963.

Fabre, J. Henri. *The Insect World of J. Henri Fabre,* ed. Edwin Way Teale. New York: Dodd, Mead & Co., 1949.

Free, John, and Butler, Colin. *Bumblebees.* New York: The Macmillan Company, 1959.

Hoyt, Murray. *The World of Bees.* New York: Coward-McCann, 1965.

Hutchins, Ross E. *Insects: Hunters and Trappers.* New York: Rand McNally & Co., 1957.

Hylander, Clarence J. *Insects on Parade.* New York: The Macmillan Company, 1957.

Jaques, H. E. *How to Know the Insects.* 2nd ed. Dubuque, Iowa: William C. Brown Company, Publishers, 1947.

Larson, Mervin W., and Larson, Peggy. *All About Ants.* New York: The World Publishing Company, 1965.

Matheson, Robert. *Entomology for Introductory Courses.* 2nd ed. Ithaca, N.Y.: Comstock Publishing Associates, 1951.

Oldroyd, Harold. *The Natural History of Flies.* New York: W. W. Norton & Company, 1965.

Oman, P. W., and Cushman, A. D. *Collection and Preservation of Insects. U.S.D.A. Miscellaneous Publication 601.* Washington, D.C.: Government Printing Office, 1946.

Stefferud, Alfred. *Insects, The Yearbook of Agriculture.* Washington, D.C.: Government Printing Office, 1952.

Teale, E. W. *Grassroot Jungles.* Rev. ed. New York: Dodd, Mead & Co., 1944.

Wigglesworth, V. B. *The Life of Insects.* Cleveland, Ohio: The World Publishing Company, 1964.